CREDIT SECRETS

Author: Frankie Brackett

Discover The Ultimate Guide to Learn Credit Secrets to Finally Achieve Your Financial Freedom. Boost Your Score and Repair Your Negative Profile Legally and Quickly to Get New Loans

© **Copyright 2021 - All rights reserved.**

The content contained within this book may not be reproduced, duplicated or transmitted without direct written permission from the author or the publisher.

Under no circumstances will any blame or legal responsibility be held against the publisher, or author, for any damages, reparation, or monetary loss due to the information contained within this book. Either directly or indirectly.

Legal Notice:

This book is copyright protected. This book is only for personal use. You cannot amend, distribute, sell, use, quote or paraphrase any part, or the content within this book, without the consent of the author or publisher.

Disclaimer Notice:

Please note the information contained within this document is for educational and entertainment purposes only. All effort has been executed to present accurate, up to date, and reliable, complete information. No warranties of any kind are declared or implied. Readers acknowledge that the author is not engaging in the rendering of legal, financial, medical or professional advice. The content within this book has been derived from various sources. Please consult a licensed professional before attempting any techniques outlined in this book.

By reading this document, the reader agrees that under no circumstances is the author responsible for any losses, direct or indirect, which are incurred as a result of the use of information contained within this document, including, but not limited to, — errors, omissions, or inaccuracies.

Table of Contents

Introduction 5

Chapter 1. Most Important Things to Know About Credit Repair 6

Chapter 2. Fair Credit Reporting Act 11

Chapter 3. Section 609 16

Chapter 4. The FICO Credit Scores 22

Chapter 5. Look for Errors in the Report 28

Chapter 6. Why People Need Credit Repair 31

Chapter 7. What Is Credit Piggybacking 37

Chapter 8. What the Lawyers Don't Want You to Know 41

Chapter 9. How Credit Cards Effect Your Score 45

Chapter 10. Debt-Snowball Method 51

Chapter 11. How to Overcome Credit Card Debt? 55

Chapter 12. How to Fix Your Credit Yourself in 9 Easy Steps? 60

Chapter 13. How to Maintain It and Mindset 65

Chapter 14. How to Remove Extra Names and Addresses from Your Report? 71

Chapter 15. Delete Inquiries Like the Pros 75

Chapter 16. The FUQ'S (Frequently Unasked Questions): Things Everyone Should Know About Their Credit Score..................79

Chapter 17. How to Protect Your Credit and Credit Monitoring?..................85

Chapter 18. Reach Your Financial Freedom..................88

Chapter 19. Template Examples and Simulations..................94

Conclusion..................103

Introduction

First, let's start with what credit is exactly. Credit refers to money that has been borrowed by an individual or a company. When somebody borrows money, they are then said to have "borrowed" the money from someone else; other people who want their money back typically do this through lenders who have agreed on terms when lending them the funds--this person would be called a "lender" or "investor." Credit can be obtained from many sources, and it is also very easy to get.

The first step to take when you think you need credit repair is understanding what kind of credit problem you have. This is so Credit Secret can help you build your Credit Score.

Your credit reports and scores will vary by the credit bureau, which means that each bureau will have its own unique information about you and your credit history. Your credit reports may also vary over time as you and your debt situation change.

Your Score may vary by the credit bureau. Each credit bureau has its own unique scoring criteria. The exact score calculation changes daily and is based on the most up-to-date information in your credit report from each bureau.

Those who want to make money through cash back or rewards programs must first understand that there are many different sorts of rewards programs. There is a program for everyone whether it's an airline mile, hotel points, groceries, or free nights. The good news is this is also where we can make some money for ourselves with our credit cards when we know how to efficiently utilize them. If you're looking to get the most out of your credit cards, it's important to either use credit cards that don't charge fees for all of your purchases or a card that has a low interest rate. Credit card companies are making it easier for consumers to not have to choose one feature over the other but instead choose a card that has both features and also provides them with rewards. These features can include cashback or points cards.

Chapter 1. Most Important Things to Know About Credit Repair

With poor credit, navigating today's world is challenging. A lot of businesses use your credit to choose whether or not to conduct business with you, as well as to determine the price of goods and services you use.

Credit restoration is often sought by consumers with a poor credit background in order to boost their financial status. Here are the most important items to consider when you evaluate your choices.

1. You Can Do It Yourself

Although hiring a reputable credit repair company can be a choice for others, there really is nothing they can do for you that you can't do yourself. There is a lot of information in books and on the website that you can use to inform yourself on how credit functions and what you can do to improve your credit.

Negative information may be deleted from the credit report through methods such as credit report disputes, pay for deletion, debt validation, and goodwill notes, which are all tactics used by credit repair companies to erase negative information.

Not only can doing it yourself save you money, but it will also allow you more strength and control of your credit history. If you have learned how to fix credit, you will be able to use them if it's required in the future.

2. It pertains to your credit report rather than your credit score

The details on your credit report have an effect on the credit score. This is why the first move in fixing your credit is to update your credit report.

Visit AnnualCreditReport.com to receive a complimentary sample of your credit check from one of the three credit bureaus TransUnion, Experian, and Equifax.

Tip: Due to the COVID-19 pandemic, free credit reviews are now accessible every week rather than a year from AnnualCreditReport.com.

3. Your credit score indicates where your credit stand

Keep an eye on your credit score; it will indicate if your credit is fine, negative, or improving. A low credit score denotes a credit background that needs to be improved. It's a sign that your credit background is changing as your credit score rises.

Buying your credit report any time you want to check where you stand will quickly add up. You can monitor your credit improvement for free by using a free credit score platform like Credit Sesame or Credit Karma.

Look for a credit management program that does not use a credit card when you sign up. Otherwise, you could be signed up for the free trial subscription that would start billing you every month if you don't cancel the plan.

It is critical to note: Payment background, debt number, credit history, age, credit account forms, and recent credit applications are all factors that go into determining the credit score. Your credit score would rise as you improve your credit in any of these areas.

4. It's Difficult to Get Rid of Accurate Negative Information

It's worth noting that the word "accurate" is capitalized. Only lawfully obligated credit bureaus are required to erase misleading or unverifiable records from your credit report.

It's more difficult to remove correctly recorded negative details from the credit report, and the credit bureaus are all within their rights to do so. In fact, credit bureaus must report all accurate information, including negative information, for the credit system to function properly.

A settlement account on a debt you owe is one of the various strategies to get rid of incorrect negative records. These methods can take longer and require more work than a simple credit report disagreement. The better choices for these forms of accounts are debt validation (for settlement agencies), pay for removal, and goodwill deletion requests.

5. It's Possible That Doing Nothing Is a Strategy

Negative details would not last forever on the credit report. The majority of negative details on your credit report will be removed after seven years. There're a few exceptions to this rule. Unpaid tax liens and bankruptcy will sit on the credit record for up to ten years.

If an account is approaching the credit reporting period limit, waiting for this to fall off could be less frustrating and time-consuming than attempting to remove it using dispute letters or other methods.

Taking action on a bad record would not increase the credit reporting period limit, contrary to common opinion. For example, whether you pay off a six-year-old debt record, it would not be removed from the credit history after seven years.

Notice that paying collections are not included with certain recent versions of the VantageScore and FICO credit scores.

6. Closing Accounts Isn't Going to Help

It's a common misconception that only active accounts are used on a person's credit report and that closing an account would erase it. Unfortunately, closing an account may have a negative impact on your credit report in certain situations.

It is not possible to remove an account from your credit report by closing it. The information regarding the closed account, as stated by your creditors, may remain on your credit report. Furthermore, closing a credit card account will lower a person's credit use and will have a negative impact on their credit score.

In an email interview with the balance, Nancy Bistritz Balkan, earlier Director Public Relations & Communications of Global Customer Solutions at Equifax, states, "Before closing accounts, customers can take into account other considerations that compose credit ratings, such as the amount of time the account has been available." Equifax is one of the three major credit bureaus. "If you have shown the correct kinds of behavior for an account over a set amount of time (i.e., payment on time every time), closing the account may not make sense."

Leaving the account open will actually help you restore your score, whether it is in good standing or can be taken back into good standing by paying off the past due balance. You'll need open, active accounts with a strong payment history to improve your credit score. For a poor credit score, opening new accounts may be tough, but rehabilitating the accounts you still have open can be far easier.

7. Credit repair firms are always untrustworthy.

Often credit repair businesses offer lofty commitments they can't keep, charge advance rates, and then refuse to perform. Both of these are prohibited under federal legislation, but customers who are unaware of the law do not know they are being used until it is too late.

The Federal Trade Commission has been pursuing scores of credit repair firms who have violated the rules over the last few years. These businesses are often fined and, in certain circumstances, prohibited from doing service in the credit repair sector.

The below are few red flags if you're engaging with a shady credit repair company: they demand payment in advance before any services are provided, claim a government affiliation or exclusive relationship with the credit bureaus, promise a particular credit score, promise to exclude correct info from your credit report, failure to advise you of your right to dispute relevant information with the credit bureaus or ask you to include personal information.

8. Don't Expect Immediate Results

Rebuilding a poor credit history requires time. Your more recent credit history weighs in more heavily on your credit score than older items.

A decent credit background would usually have few negative entries and a lot of recent favorable credit records. A couple of months of on-time payments is a good start, but it won't immediately get you excellent credibility. Your credit can steadily increase when the bad information drops off or becomes older, and you substitute it with better information.

As the details in your credit report updates throughout the credit repair phase, your credit score can fluctuate. Instead of focusing on frequent variations, consider the overall pattern of your credit score over time.

9. Change Your Habits to Secure Your Improved Credit Score

Many citizens go through credit repair, whether they manage it themselves or hire a company—in order to be able to borrow money, such as for a mortgage or a car loan. This is not a problem at all.

However, if you really want good credit to last, you must build credit-building behaviors. This involves borrowing just as much as you can expect to repay (and might be even a little less). One of the easiest things you can do with your reputation is to pay the bills on time.

According to Bistritz Balkan, "A good rule of thumb to note when it comes to creditworthiness is to settle the bills on time every time. Lenders and borrowers deserve to see that you've always met your contractual obligations on schedule. As a result, paying bills on time is a critical, early-on habit to acquire."

Chapter 2.   Fair Credit Reporting Act

Credit reporting is a financial service that provides information about the credit history of individuals. A credit report is compiled based on the individual's creditors, public records, and financial statements. There are three major U.S. credit reporting agencies-- Equifax, Experian, and TransUnion-- that generate reports for banks to use in qualifying an individual for a loan or other form of credit.

The Fair Credit Reporting Act (FCRA) was enacted by Congress in 1970 to establish procedures intended to ensure accurate and fair collection of consumer information by CRAs working within the scope of their responsibilities under Section 603(f) of Title 15 United States Code (the Consumer Credit Protection Act or "CCPA").

In 1978, Congress reacted to the experience of the Watergate scandal where political operatives successfully manipulated consumer credit files in an effort to undermine their opponents. In response, it enacted the FCRA, which gave consumers more rights over their information.

The FCRA established federal standards for credit reporting agencies. The statute requires that consumer reports contain specific items of information and that they be updated only as described by law. Any person who uses a credit report to deny an individual access to credit is subject to a $1,000 penalty for each instance.

Further, the FCRA includes a number of important consumer rights. It requires that all consumer reports be accurate and kept current. It also requires that the CRAs notify consumers of any error in their files, correct any inaccuracies, and notify them/the individual if their report contains information about him/her that is false or misleading.

The individual has the right to request his/her credit report within 60 days from the date it was received by the CRA. The CRA must furnish all requested information on request without further charge. The CRA must investigate all information contained in a consumer report pertaining to the individual that it furnished to another person. The CRA must notify any individual who is identified as having information contained in their report which is false. The agency will then allow the individual an opportunity to challenge any information contained in their file, and if false, the item must be deleted. If the CRA fails to complete an investigation within 30 days of receipt of a complete investigation request, they have up to 60 days to investigate. A consumer can invoke these procedures for one free copy of his/her report per year if they are unemployed and intend on applying for employment within 60 days or for a specific credit transaction (e.g., applying for an amount greater than $50).

Credit reports can also play an important in the employer-employee relationship. According to the Equal Employment Opportunity Commission, employers may obtain consumer reports, but only as a part of a legitimate hiring process or for a legitimate business purpose.

Generally speaking, employment applications will include an authorization for employers to obtain a credit report and the employee must be provided with their credit report before making any decision such as hiring or promoting the employee. Employers may not base employment decisions solely on information found in the report.

Employers must also have signed documentation from the employee authorizing them to order his/her credit report and proof that they were given their authorization to do so before ordering it.

Further, placing an employee's job on hold during the 60-day period following a request for a credit report is unlawful.

If the employer requests information from the CRA that they have not already provided to another person, that request must include a reasonable and good faith effort to notify the individual whose information is sought.

Credit reporting agencies may only share information about the customers with their subsidiaries and other companies within an industry group, and only if it serves a business purpose. If there are less than 400 employees in any one location, CRAs may not share any of its customers' personal data with its subsidiaries or other companies within 250 miles (400 kilometers) of headquarters.

A credit report is a financial statement prepared in advance of a loan or other form of credit. It is designed to provide information about the individual's creditworthiness to potential creditors and potential users of the information. The purpose of the report is to allow creditors and users to determine an individual's ability to repay debt.

Credit reports are used primarily by banks, mortgage lenders, money managers, insurance companies, and retailers when evaluating loan or credit applicants:

When a business decides it needs additional money secured by real estate, stocks, or bonds, it will want to know if the person who wants to borrow that money has enough income or assets from which the business can raise capital. The business will request a loan or credit report. The report will be prepared by a credit reporting agency, which gathers information from the individual's bank, employers, creditors, and others about how much money the individual receives and what the individual owes. The agency records this information on the individual's "credit report," which is sent to the potential creditor or lender for review before extending credit.

Credit reporting agencies have existed in Canada since 1910 when agencies began monitoring consumer debt payments. In 1968, the federal government passed legislation to protect Canadians from abuse of their files via a new Credit Reporting Act (CRA). The new legislation was created to ensure that credit reports were accurate and used fairly.

One of the major initiatives of the CRA was to establish a Privacy Code for Credit Reporting Agencies, or the "Code." This Code, which is now enforced by the federal Office of the Privacy Commissioner of Canada (OPC), "establishes provisions for fair information practices relating to consumer reporting." The provisions in the Code are designed "to protect consumer privacy in an era of increasingly complex credit transactions and rapid advances in technology.

The Code is divided into four main objectives:

1. The fundamental objective of all businesses involved in credit reporting is to provide information on consumers that is accurate, complete, and up-to-date
2. Credit reporting agencies in Canada are responsible for gathering accurate information on consumers, and for establishing the legal grounds to collect, use and disclose personal information contained in credit reports.
3. The Code ensures that the personal information from credit reports is legally obtained (not stolen or illegally accessed) and that it is used appropriately. It also ensures that individuals are treated fairly by all parties involved in the credit reporting process.
4. The Code establishes guidelines for the use of personal information, including the collection of such information by a business, transfer of such information to third parties, and disclosure of personal information to others. This legislation also ensures that those who handle this sensitive data cannot abuse it or use it inappropriately.

The following are the most significant provisions of the Code:

1. It is important to note that the Code does not cover all aspects of credit reporting. It deals solely with consumer credit reports and excludes information relating to commercial credit or certain insurance-related information. For more information, see these related links:

Filing a report about an individual with a credit reporting agency is itself an act that may constitute an offense if it is done in bad faith (e.g., for the purpose of harassing someone). Additionally, filing a false report can be an offense (Section 322(2) of the Federal Criminal Code).

The Department of Justice Canada has investigated and taken action against 29 federally regulated entities for alleged violations under the new legislation. Some of these cases are examples of how broadly the legislation is being enforced:

In the early 1990s, credit reporting agencies began to use national real names and full addresses as identifiers on credit files. This was in contrast to the 1970s, when no genuine names were utilized. The use of full names was a compounding problem because it made it difficult to protect privacy. A real name cannot be secret so there was always a risk that it would be disclosed by accident or due to an inadvertent error. This is especially concerning for those who are vulnerable, such as children and the elderly.

The federal government implemented a new policy in the early 2000s that required real names to be removed from all but the most recent credit files. This made it difficult for people to maintain their privacy as growing numbers of institutions began to use real names as identifiers on their own computer systems.

In 2015, Canada's privacy commissioner, Daniel Therrien, recommended that full address information not be included in credit files and that it should be removed from all other personal data systems maintained by the federal government. His recommendation was based on studies that found that about half of the people affected were elderly and many did not have access to a computer.

He also recommended that the federal government should issue regulations requiring institutions to take measures to ensure that information was de-identified prior to being used in decisions about lending.

In April 2017, the federal privacy commissioner, Daniel Therrien, issued new guidelines for the use of personal data for making decisions on lending. His new guidelines follow on from his 2015 recommendations about protections for personal data in credit files. According to Therrien, it is essential that personal information in credit files is protected against misrepresentation and misuse while maintained by third parties such as banks and government agencies.

Chapter 3. Section 609

What Is the Credit Dispute 609 Letter?

You may remove negative items from the credit report based on Section 609. A lot of people have been successful in the process, boosting their credit score. The process involves a written letter asking for the verification of every piece of information in your file hoping that something wasn't properly documented.

If the creditor failed to document something properly, no legal choice is there but to remove the negative items from the credit report.

How Does A 609 Letter Work?

Now that you've reviewed your credit reports, credit scores, and credit history, you're ready to start thinking about what you can do to start pushing it upwards. Take each category of the FICO credit score, look at your history, and ask how you can improve that category.

You should begin by grouping problems you identified from your credit report review in a way that makes the most sense to you.

Consider creating a separate email account for your credit rating efforts. It will make it easier to keep related emails organized.

Here's one approach to organizing your tasks:

1. Quick and easy

If you have some credit inquiries that will expire soon, there's nothing you need to do except be careful about applying for new credit. Using some of your savings to reduce your debt load on a credit card that's near its limit is pretty simple, so long as you have the money to do so.

2. Moderate effort

If you found any discrepancies in any of your credit reports, you should contact the appropriate credit reporting company to see if you can get the error corrected. Remember, both the credit reporting companies and creditors are responsible for correcting inaccurate or incomplete information in your credit report, according to the FTC. Each of the three companies concerned has web pages specifically for customer disputes.

3. More effort

You can probably get a creditor to remove a late payment from your account record (more on this in a few lines). Another strategy you can consider is to take out a debt consolidation loan (more on this in a few lines too). It's a riskier strategy, so it needs to be carefully considered. If you've found a discrepancy in your credit report, writing a letter to the responsible credit reporting company should be one of the first things you do. The FTC even provides you with a sample letter on its website. The FTC recommends you send the letter via certified mail "return receipt requested." It also says to include copies (not originals) of any relevant documents or receipts you have. It can also help send a copy of the page from your credit report with the item(s) circled.

While you can probably get things done via company websites, going the paper route gives you a physically documented record of your efforts. While you hopefully won't need it, hard evidence can be easier to work with and be more reliable than electronic records.

Get Your Stuff Together

It helps to be organized. Create a binder or file and start gathering any records that will help you make your case with the various companies you're going to need to communicate with. Make sure you have either websites or email addresses for your creditors. Small businesses might not offer much when it comes to websites, but you can count on the major credit card companies to have functional websites that include ways to contact them for help or disputes. They usually have live support available online too. Remember, if you're communicating in real-time, be prepared ahead of time and have at least an outline of what you want to cover in your call. It is one advantage of using the mail to make your dispute, and you're much more likely to submit all the necessary proof. Make sure you have the originals of everything before you send in your dispute.

Your Checklist

Put together a checklist with deadlines to help keep you on track. Organize by the approach you like best. You can go from easy to hard, get going on the stuff that will take longer to respond on, and then knock off the faster stuff, so while the slow-moving chores are winding their way through the mail or a company bureaucracy, you can be getting things done.

Removing late payment codes: try to get as many of these removed as you can. Late payments take seven years to clear from your credit history, so trying to get as many as you can be removed can be a big help.

Correcting errors: If you are correcting misspellings, incorrect information, and erroneous accounts. Credit bureaus have 30 days to investigate your complaint. You can use the mail system or website for Equifax or TransUnion. Experian only accepts requests online. You can find phone numbers, web addresses, and mail addresses for each company (if offered) here. One thing to look at extra strictly is anything listed by collections agencies. Consumer debt has a legal expiration date. Once that date has passed, you can't be forced to pay it. Collection agencies can still attempt to collect that debt, and they can even sell the debt to other collectors who will then try their luck collecting the debt. In the process, the dates recorded for that debt can be misreported, requiring correction. Of course, if a debt collector contacted you and you agreed to pay anything back (whether you paid any money or not), the clock on the debt begins from that point on.

Reducing debt ratios on credit cards: try to avoid having any tickets that are near their limits if you can. Considering transferring a balance if you can do so without doing anything to make your report worse (such as applying for a new card to shift the balance). Paying down the cards is ideal if you have the money.

Disputing items: this is a little different than correcting errors. Here, you're trying to get things off your report that may be justified. Still, if you can convince the creditor to remove the item, it's to your advantage, and let's face it, it's not like you're going to bully a big credit card company into doing something it doesn't want to do. Even disputing an old negative charge can sometimes pay off simply because the creditor may not respond.

Clearing civil judgments: these also appear on your credit history, so if you can pay them off or get them discharged, it will benefit your credit score.

Does a 609 Letter Improve My Credit?

While one's economic situation is different from another person's, most people may be in some debt at a particular time. For instance, you may have small debts such as in-store financing or credit card bills, while others may have large ones such as mortgages and loans. This translates that almost everyone is most likely dependent on having a specific amount of credit. Confidence can be useful for some things.

As mentioned earlier, your credit report, which is held by a credit bureau, is significant to your credit status.

The credit bureau will send you a notification when you are in default or missed payments to your creditors. Once you receive such notices, expect that you are in for a poor credit rating.

There are various steps involved in effective credit repair. These steps are particular to the situation of an individual. One of the most common actions that people in a bad credit situation take is debt consolidation.

If you are attempting to have your credit repaired, it is a principle to act as quickly as possible. Once you miss out on payments to your creditors, your credit rating will be damaged almost immediately. The more you continuously miss your payments, the more damaged your credit rating will be.

You might be one of the numerous people who get confused that credit is simply "good" or "bad," and once you are in trouble with a creditor, it is a futile effort to repair it. On the contrary, even if you are in a bad credit situation, credit repair enables you to pay off your debts in the quickest way possible. However, most people avoid any credit repair strategies because, first of all, they do not have money to pay their debts. For instance, you may have an unfortunate economic situation, which is why you missed out on your payments. This is the reason why a debt consolidation is an efficient tool, which can help you in repairing your credit.

Debt consolidation, as the name implies, consolidates all your debts into just one loan. This means that if you have outstanding debts from various creditors, you can secure a loan from just one company and use the loan amount to pay your outstanding debts. You will only make your payments on a single loan and a single creditor/company.

Through debt consolidation, you will be able to have flexibility when your debts are already unmanageable. While you would still owe the same amount of money, debt consolidation allows you to secure a loan over the long term to lower your monthly payments.

Furthermore, debt consolidation will enable you to improve your relationship with your creditors and paves the way for repairing your credit. Through debt consolidation, your creditors will report to credit bureaus that your debts are already cleared up; thus, the credit repair process can start quickly.

Ultimately, debt consolidation changes your status with your creditors in a quick manner. It stops the damage to your financial situation before it gets worse.

You can be on good terms with just a single creditor as compared to being on bad terms with multiple ones. Besides, debt consolidation allows you to breathe before engaging in credit repair.

What Is in Section 609, You Have the Right to Request

This works by first disputing with the credit report authorities legitimately. Each credit authority has a connection to discuss any of your credit things so you can do this on the web if you wish, or you can submit one recorded as a hard copy by sending them a letter.

Occasionally, a credit report office may evacuate after your first question or dispute. Often, however, you will be required to catch up with further documentation. For instance, if a report contains an equalization mistake, you may need to send receipts or other verification that shows why you trust it is off base.

The Credit Departments' Duty

A significant part of the duty regarding exact announcing falls on the credit report authorities. That is the reason why the questioning procedure begins with them. As indicated by the FCRA, credit report organizations are required to remember just exact and unquestionable data for your credit report. This implies that if the credit agency does not get palatable reactions from your loan bosses, they are committed to expelling any negatives from your credit report.

Chapter 4.   The FICO Credit Scores

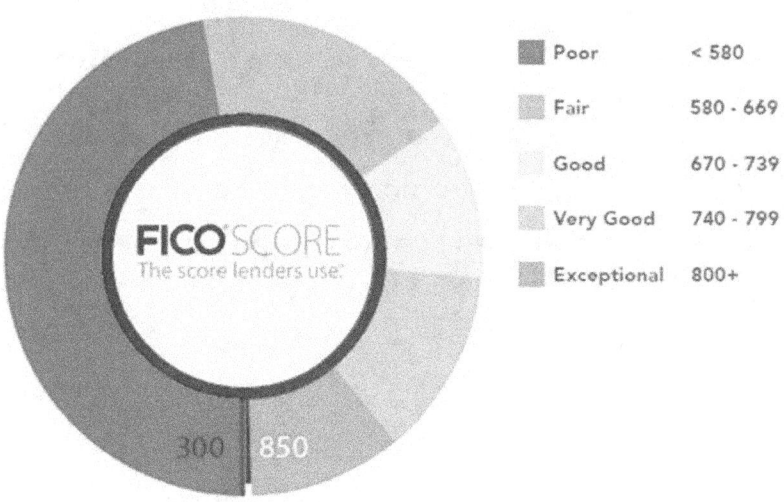

You must have heard about the term FICO when you are talking about credit score. It is one of the very popular methods of credit scoring that is done by Fair Issacs Corporation or FICO. When a lender is lending you money, they will want to check what your FICO score is and several other things that are usually mentioned in your credit report so that they can assess how much risk is there in lending you money and whether they should extend credit or not. There are several factors that are considered before the FICO score is calculated. Some of them are types of credit used, payment history, new credit accounts, credit history length, and your current state of indebtedness.

Now, FICO is basically an analytics software company. The name of the company was Fair Issacs Corporation, but the name was changed in the year 2009 and the credit scores that this company produces are the ones that are most widely used. And when you approach a financial institution for borrowing money, they will use these scores to decide whether to lend you money or not.

The scores usually are given between 300 and 850. You'll know that your credit history is good if the score is above 650, and on the other hand, if it is less than 620, then borrowing money will be a difficult task. As compared to other scoring models, FICO is the one that is more popularly used. If you check with the mortgage sector, you will see that so many people have a stringent rule of a minimum FICO score in order to get approval. That is also the reason why people give FICO the maximum attention and try to maintain their FICO score above all other scores.

I think you have already heard multiple times that your FICO score should be this or that, and only then will you get the credit you want. So, this score definitely gains weightage among the common people. But not everyone understands what it is and what its importance is. Since this number is so important, more and more people should be aware of what it is instead of simply going with the flow or accepting that the FICO score is important.

How Can You Calculate FICO Scores?

If you think that anyone can know how the FICO scores are calculated then no, it doesn't happen that way. The company keeps it a secret and so they never release any details regarding how the score is actually calculated. It's basically a secret formula. Also, the scores are not produced by the company. There is software that has been produced by the company and the same software is used by TransUnion, Experian, and Equifax – the major credit bureaus. The formula of FICO is used by all three bureaus where they input their data into the formula to obtain the results. But there is something about all of this and that is – a general outline has been given by FICO so that consumers can know which entities are weighted and used and we are going to discuss them here –

1. Payment History – This is about whether you have been paying your credits timely or not. Each line of credit will be clearly mentioned in your credit report, and if you had paid them late, then that will be mentioned too. For example, if you had made the payment 30 or 60 or even 120 days late, then that will be clearly mentioned. This accounts for 35% of the total score.

2. Accounts Owed – Having a debt is not at all good, and this is something that we all can probably agree upon. This is all about the amount of money you owe to someone. But, on the contrary, you have to understand that your credit scores will not automatically become low just because you have low debt. Instead, what is considered is the ratio between the credit available and the amount of money owed. For example, if a person owes $20000 and at the same, all his credit cards have reached their maximum drawing limit and all the credits have been fully extended, then that person's credit score is going to be really low as compared to someone who has a debt of $80000 but none of his accounts have reached the limit. This will account for 30% of the total score.
3. Credit Mix – As the name suggests, it means it checks the variety of accounts that a person has. If you want your credit score to be good, then your mix of accounts should be strong like mortgages, credit cards, various retail accounts, and vehicle loans. This will account for 10% of the score.
4. Credit History Length – In general terms, your credit score will automatically be good if your credit history is long. But this actually varies in certain cases. If the situation is in favor, then you can have a good score even with a credit history that is short. This will account for 15% of the score.
5. New Credit – If you have any accounts that have been recently opened, that is referred to as new credit. If you have had recently opened several accounts in a time span that is considerably short, then your score will automatically be lowered because of the high risk involved. This accounts for 10% of the total score.

All about the Versions of FICO

Since the calculations of the FICO are being updated ever since its existence, that is why the company keeps releasing newer versions periodically. The base version of the FICO score calculation was released in the year 1989. Whenever a newer version is released, all the lenders are free to use it to their will. Also, whether a lender wants to upgrade it to the latest version or not is completely their choice, and so, it is not mandatory.

Version 8 or FICO 8 was released in the year 2009. One of the best things about this version is that the score is predictable because of the unique features that were introduced to the base score algorithm.

The main idea of a FICO score remains the same in all its versions, and that is to show the borrower that they have to be responsible with debt and interact accordingly. If you have been paying your bills and loan EMIs on time, then your scores will automatically be high. You should also maintain your credit card balances low and you should not recklessly open any new accounts until and unless you have a targeted purchase in mind. On the contrary, if you are someone who faces delinquency very frequently, then you are bound to have lower scores. So, you should never be frivolous with any credit decisions that you make. The FICO 8 ignored those collection accounts completely in which a minimum balance of $100 was not present.

Highly utilizer credit cards were given a greater level of sensitivity in the FICO 8. In simpler terms, if you are a borrower, then your score will be positively affected if your active credit cards have low balances. When compared to the past versions of FICO, all the late payments have been treated only after good judgment. So, if your late payment was just an isolated event and the rest of your financial life is in order, then your score will not be affected because of it. Also, for representing risk in a better way that is statistically clearer, there are more categories of consumers shown in FICO 8. This was done mostly because previously, those who had a robust credit history were judged on the same curve as those who had almost no credit history at all. But this change actually made the two categories separate.

In the year 2016, FICO score of 9 was released, and there are some minor adjustments to the things mentioned in score 8 with respect to rental history sensitivity, medical collection accounts, and also it is now seen with forgiving eyes when there is a third- party collection that is fully paid. But till date, the FICO 9 has not been started in any of the major credit bureaus.

Industry-Specific FICO Scores

Sometimes the FICO scores are optimized so that they can be perfect for a product belonging to a particular industry. Some examples are credit cards and auto loans. The base Fico score versions and the industry-specific FICO scores have the same foundation, but since every industry has its own risk, that is why these scores have been designed to match those. The main benefit is that the lenders who are lending the money have the most updated information at their hands. This helps them in making the best decisions so that the borrowers are getting the right credit.

The likelihood of a borrower not paying the money in full in the future, which is the usual thing to do, is measured by the base FICO score. It can be a student loan, credit card, or even a mortgage. But in the case of industry FICO scores has the features of the base scores but in addition to that, it also performs a more finely tuned risk assessment of that particular industry and this score is perfectly tailored for any particular type of credit. For example, a FICO Bankcard Score is for a credit card whereas a FICO Auto Score is for auto lenders.

So, people often get confused about what type of FICO score should they be looking into and that is why I have come up with a very clear guide for you.

If you are planning to get a car on financing, the FICO Auto Scores are what you are going to need. For a credit evaluation, these scores will have the upper hand.

Similarly, if you are going to apply for a new credit card, then it is not only the base FICO score that will be used by the lenders but also your FICO Bankcard Score.

In the case of credit evaluations in the mortgage sector, the versions of FICO scores that were present before version 8 are the ones that are mostly used. You should have an idea of them as well.

The base FICO Score 8 is the one that is most commonly used in cases like retail credit, student loans, and personal loans.

Another common question that most people have is that whether closing their credit would help them improve their FICO Score 8 but no, it's not going to be of any help, because a reported closed status of a credit card is not considered in the FICO score. But if the closed account had any record of missed payments even if it was in the past, it will be considered against your score.

Also, you should be aware of the fact that even though it is the FICO score that is more popularly used, there is another score table that is rising in popularity, and that is the Vantage Score. Almost 10% of the companies are now using it. The process of calculation of this score is quite different from that of FICO. In the case of Vantage Score, the payment history comprises 40% of the score, credit used accounts for 20%, type of credit and age accounts for 21%, any recent queries or credit behavior accounts for 5%, available credit accounts for 3%, and your total debt or balance accounts for 11%.

Chapter 5. Look for Errors in the Report

If I had to mention one thing you should do when you get your credit report, it is reading it front to back. I know that might sound like a daunting task but most people skip over the fine print and miss important information. You need to have someone who will go through the report with a fine-toothed comb. It is also wise not to over-extend yourself, and if your credit score isn't in the sky-high numbers then don't use that as an excuse for making rash decisions about what debts you want or need to take on."

Keeping your credit score high can be hard work but not impossible if you work hard at it. One great way to lower your credit score is by not paying your bills on time. Bad credit will be the result of not paying bills on time and you will want to avoid this at all costs. There are clues that you need to look for so that you can prevent these types of problems from happening.

Your credit report is actually more complicated than it may appear at first glance, simply because you are dealing with reports from three different agencies, TransUnion, Experian, and Equifax. What this means is that you will need to check each of the three reports on a regular basis to ensure you have all the pertinent information on your current credit score.

A credit report includes your credit history, payment information, and public records. It's a snapshot of how you manage your finances. Your credit score is derived from this information, which creditors use to determine whether you're a safe borrower.

What are the benefits of reading my credit report?
Reading your own credit report can save time and money by identifying errors in the report before applying for loans or insurance policies that could be denied based on false information. This will also help to understand how much interest you may have to pay on certain loans because some lenders base their rates off of accurate information found in a consumer's credit reports or scores.

Anatomy of a credit report

While the three major credit reports are going to vary somewhat, information is always going to be grouped into four major categories, these are credit inquires, creditor information, public record information, and personal information.

Personal information: The personal information section is going to include things like your name and any aliases you use, your social security number, date of birth, employment information, and your current and previous addresses.

Public record information: This section will include any currently pending legal issues related to your current financial situation. This can include bankruptcies, wage garnishments, judgments, and liens. A TransUnion report will also show the approximate date when these details will be removed from your report.

Creditor Information: This section will show all of your debts that have been turned over to a collection agency and all of the lines of credit that you currently have. Additionally, you will find details outlining the status of the account in question, if you share responsibility on any of the accounts, your current balance, payment history, credit limit, and if the account is currently past due. Typically, positive and negative accounts will be grouped together.

If you have accounts that are negatively affecting your credit, it is important to keep in mind that you can dispute any of these issues with the credit reporting company. Barring that they will fall off your report after the issue has been resolved for seven years.

Each of your accounts can be classified in the following ways: if any of your accounts are listed as charged off, that means that the account has been written off from the creditor as a loss. While this means you may not have to pay off the account, it will still show up on your credit report for seven years. A revolving account is a classification given to credit cards, you don't need to pay these in full each month and can instead revolve them and just pay the interest.

An installment account is a classification given to loans or other accounts that involved fixed payments. An open account is a classification given to accounts that force you to pay the total balance off each month. A collection account is a classification given to any account that has been transferred to a debt collection agency, this will even show on accounts that you have settled the debt for in the past seven years.

Credit inquiries: This section of your credit report includes a list of every agency that has reviewed your credit report in the past seven years. There are two different types of inquiries, hard inquiries are made by lenders when you apply for a line of credit, too many of these in a seven-year period can negatively impact your credit score. Soft inquiries are made by you or agencies that preapprove you for lines of credit.

Credit report codes: The following is a list of codes you may see on your credit report and what they mean.

- CURR ACCT: This means the account is in good standing and current.
- CUR WAS 30-2: This means the account is currently in good standing but has been late by 30 days or more at least twice.
- PAID: This means the account is currently inactive and has been paid off
- CHARGOFF: This means the account has been charged off.
- COLLECT: This means the account has been sent to collections.
- BKLIQREQ: This means the debt has been forgiven due to bankruptcy.
- DELINQ 60: This means the account is at least 60 days past due.

Chapter 6. Why People Need Credit Repair

On average, Americans have about $16,000 in credit card debt and close to a trillion dollars in mortgage debt. Those staggering numbers reflect a larger trend: people are irresponsible with their money and not managing it well enough. It's no wonder that one of the most popular Google search queries is "credit score."

People need help with their financial problems and credit repair companies offer a unique solution that can help make the difference between success and failure. Credit repair companies can assist with bad debts, lower interest rates, or even erase bad debts altogether so that you can rebuild your credit once more.

It's no wonder that you need credit repair if your credit is in bad shape. The hard truth is that people need credit repair because they have bad credit scores. More than that, people need credit repair because they have FICO scores under 600, the kind of score that can wreck a person's life.

People need credit repair and it doesn't take a genius to figure out why: banks and creditors don't want to do business with you if you have poor credit. This means your options are limited when it comes to getting a loan or any type of financing in general. People need credit repair as a last resort in this scenario, but it's still an important one.

Bad Credit Reports Can Be the Difference between Success and Failure

People with bad credit reports are in an unfortunate position. When times get tough, people can find themselves in a sticky situation for one reason or another. This could mean that people don't have enough cash for an emergency expense, or they may be unable to make ends meet because their paychecks aren't what they used to be.

Regardless of the circumstances at hand, people who have bad credit reports find themselves struggling under these strains while others are able to keep calm and carry on with their lives as though nothing were wrong.

It's not fair that life isn't fair. People who have bad credit reports find themselves in trouble because of factors that aren't in their control. Taking care of your own business is an important part of life, and it extends past our personal lives as well. Credit repair companies help people keep moving forward and staying in a strong financial state so that they can hold down a job, pay the bills, and put food on the table without worrying about how they are going to get by. Bad credit scores should never be taken lightly, which is why people need credit repair when things fall apart and they get into trouble.

As mentioned briefly above, credit repair companies can help people keep moving forward and stay in a strong financial state. If you've noticed your paycheck doesn't amount to what it used to be or that you're having trouble paying off debts – this is the time to call in a credit repair company. Credit repair companies can make the difference between success and failure, and they won't leave you out to dry when it comes to financial decisions and personal problems.

People need credit repair for one simple reason: because they have bad credit ratings. Bad credit scores reflect bad business, and businesses aren't willing to pay you money if they don't think they can get a good return. For this reason, people need credit repair so that they can keep their jobs or even find new ones altogether.

People need credit repair when they have bad scores because banks won't give them loans. People who have bad scores are hurting because they aren't able to get the financing that could lead to more opportunities for success, such as buying a car or even a house! Credit repair companies help people keep moving forward despite their obstacles, which is why people need credit repair on a regular basis.

Credit scores are important to people's lives because they reflect all of a person's financial history. This includes loans, credit card accounts, and other types of credit that a person may have paid on over the years. With this kind of information, people can see how much money they have put on the line in their lives – it's often not as much as they would like to make in case, they lose their job or take a pay cut.

It's no wonder that people need credit repair when they have a bad credit score. If you've noticed your paychecks aren't the same or that you can't seem to get a loan for a car or house, it's time to call in a credit repair company because failing to act could mean losing out on opportunities or even hurting your position in the job market.

Bad scores reflect poor business – so it makes sense that people need credit repair when they have bad FICO scores. When a person's FICO score is low, it means that he or she will have a harder time getting approved for business loans. In fact, people with bad credit scores might find they are unable to get approved for things like student loans or even credit based on their past financial history.

Despite the fact that bad credit scores can affect one's financial well-being negatively, many people still fail to realize how important their scores can be to their future success. Bad scores can result in missed opportunities because banks won't give loans to people who have poor credit, and it also hurts one's social standing because some organizations will want higher quality applicants (usually those with good credit) for their jobs.

People need credit repair on a regular basis because they have poor credit. Just like you can't start a new diet without going back to your old ways, you can't begin a new financial year without going back to your old ways. This is why people need credit repair so that they can continue working toward their positive financial future. Ideally, people who want to be successful will reach out for help and use the services of a reputable and experienced credit repair company.

When people ignore their credit, it can have a negative impact on their financial future. No matter how hard they try to fix their credit by themselves, it becomes harder and harder to improve their scores. The best way to break out of this cycle is by calling in a professional credit repair company. These companies will help you create financial strategies that actually work – which is why people need credit repair!

Bad scores often reflect bad business because they are based on past mistakes and bad decisions. When a person has bad scores, he or she may have trouble finding new jobs because employers will want to choose from job candidates who have good scores. As a result of this, many people who have bad scores end up losing their jobs.

Because of this, people need credit repair to help them improve their financial situation and stop losing out on life's opportunities as a result of their bad credit. Even a modest improvement in your scores can make a huge difference in the way that you live your life. The sooner you take action and get credit repair, the better!

Bad scores can affect one's ability to rent an apartment or obtain student loans or mortgages because not all lenders will approve applicants based on past mistakes. One's FICO score is an important factor when applying for financing.

A person whose score falls below a certain number may be denied. Lenders are generally cautious about lending money to people who have a history of late and missed payments. Some will not extend credit unless you have an excellent credit score.

Meanwhile, those who need to buy their own homes, but are renting instead, may want to think about finding a lender that does not require a good score as a prerequisite for approval. Peer-to-peer loans are a good option.

What to Do If Your Credit Scores Are Low

There's no point in worrying about credit repair if you don't have a record of negative marks on your report. The first step is to check your credit reports from the three major agencies because these are the main factors for setting your scores.

The FICO Score is typically the most looked at by financial entities, but it will only be calculated using information from one credit bureau so you need to make sure that the reports from all three bureaus are in order.

The FICO Score typically factors in the following:

- Application – If it's a new credit card or loan, this is where lenders will look. Based on information from your application, they'll get a general idea of how you may or may not be dependable. On the flip side, if it's an established credit account, which is usually measured with three to five years of payments history, the report will determine whether you will be eligible for new credit.
- Payment History – If you have no credit history on your report, it's likely because you never made any payments. This can cause a major problem if you ever try and apply for a loan or apply for insurance. FICO scores are based on the length of time between each payment so it's important that this is as long as possible. Most major lenders will allow five years before requesting proof of income from borrowers with low scores.
- Inquiries – If you have had your credit report checked by different companies, your scores could be damaged because it's difficult to accurately measure the risk of any individual when relying on information from other sources. Inquiries into your report can show up in different places but will generally affect the overall score if they happened more than once in a one-year period. It's best to avoid having a lot of applications in the same year, but if it happens, make sure you stay on top of things by following up with each company (once in a month is fine) and consult your credit card companies if you think there was a mistake.
- Length of Credit History – The longer you have accounts on your report, the better your scores tend to be. Paying accounts regularly shows that creditors have faith in how you handle bills so they will take this into consideration when evaluating your credit worthiness. If there is an account that has been delinquent or closed for another reason, then it can be problematic and show up as negative information on your report.

- Debt – If you have no debt, then it's great for your score. The more debt you have, the worse the score will be. This is particularly true if you are late with payments and have a balance that is higher than 50 percent of your credit limit. Lenders understand that it will take time to pay off debt but they don't want a borrower to spend too much on interest if they can help it. If you're struggling to pay off a loan, try and negotiate with the lender to see if they can lower or remove the interest rate.

Chapter 7.   What Is Credit Piggybacking

Finding someone to co-sign for purchases can be a challenge within itself. People are taught fundamentally, out of dealing with the consequences of co-signing for irresponsible people, that co-signing is not a good idea. Generally, it certainly isn't a good idea to co-sign because many people cannot be trusted to protect your credit when they can use it as if it is their own. Their credit is already bad, after all. What do they have to lose?

It's known as piggybacking when someone puts you as a co-signer to their credit profile and they have good credit. This method requires a lot of trusts because the person who is willing to help is at risk of damaging their credit. The best courses in credit maintenance warn those with excellent credit profiles against becoming a co-signer. This method, however, can certainly be helpful to a person who desires to raise their credit score. In three to six months, credit scores can build 100 points or better with the help of co-signing.

Co-signers have two main concerns: 1) fraud against their excellent credit (their credit gets misused), and 2) there is nothing in it for them except for the tremendous risk they are taking.

The first concern is pivotal to your co-signer's credit card. There are two key techniques to maintaining both your credit and the person who allows you to boost your score by using theirs. This will ensure that no fraud is committed and that their credit will not be misused in any way:

1. Only stay attached to that person's credit for a maximum of 6 months, and
2. Do not use that person's credit cards or their credit lines for any purchases!

Remember, your goal is only to have that person's excellent payment history documented on your reports – not to use their credit to make purchases! Using their credit is wrong.

A solution to the second concern is to offer your potential co-signor something valuable that you want to be returned to you for collateral. There are several possibilities available to you, but make sure that what you're presenting is yours and that you have the legal right to use it as collateral.

Some examples of what to use as collateral are:

1. The title to your car
2. Expensive jewelry
3. Electronics that are up to date and in excellent condition
4. The deed to your home
5. Something of your co-signer's choice.

Your options for what to use as collateral are endless, and the exchange will be more than worth it when you see the benefits your credit received as a result. Be creative in your desire to thank that person for their help, go far beyond that person's expectations, and you may make a good impression to receive their assistance.

If your co-signor refuses, it is his or her right to do so. Remember, even with collateral, the risk is tremendous on their end, and some things may not be worth the exchange to them. The key to developing your credit is to learn how to be responsible so that you do not have to rely on any quick-fix techniques like this to get where you need to be. Responsible credit behavior, making your payments early, and organizing your credit profile to showcase your excellent behavior are always the best ways to achieve the benefits you desire.

A very simple yet effective technique for boosting your credit scores is to "piggyback" on someone else's credit history and become an Authorized User (AU) on their account.

An AU account is not like a Joint Account. With a Joint Account, both you and the primary holder can add to the credit balance, but you're also both liable for the debts.

If, for example, the primary files for bankruptcy protection, then you will be on the hook for the full balance. You should avoid Joint accounts at all costs.

With an Authorized User account, only the primary cardholder is liable for the debt. However, the trade line appears on BOTH credit reports. This is also an excellent method to begin your children's credit education.

The overnight addition to a credit's age, limit, and payment history can boost a score of hundreds of points. AU accounts are so effective for increasing credit scores that many unscrupulous credit services sell them as "Seasoned Trade lines."

First of all, buying a trade line to qualify for financing, like a home mortgage, is a fraud. You could go to jail or receive a hefty fine.

Second, FICO knows about Seasoned Trade lines and has made adjustments. When those adjustments hit the scoring model lenders use, then those trade lines will become worthless.

Third, you don't need to buy trade lines anyway. Simply ask a family member or someone you've shared an address with, to add you as an AU.

Tell them you don't need or want a card, but you want your credit score to benefit from their good credit history.

Advantages

Typically, unless you get added as an authorized user from a family member or a friend, people will want to charge you like the strategy of piggybacking on other people's positive credit accounts has become well known. It's pretty standard for people to pay to be added to positive aged trade lines, companies exist and thrive on brokering these positive accounts to clients who need a boost in credit for funding purposes. This practice is 100% legal. The primary account holder can add authorized users by simply calling their credit card companies.

(Note to non-US readers: While this works in the US, it does not work in all countries. For example, this strategy does not work in Canada.)

Disadvantages

Being added as an authorized user for someone else's card isn't always good. Their history of credit payment on that card will influence your credit score. If the primary user has defaulted on a couple of payments, it will lower your credit score. On the other hand, if the primary user makes prompt payments and maintains a low balance on the card, it will improve your credit score. The primary user's credit behavior will directly influence your credit score.

This is a strategy that could backfire if the original holder of the account does not make the monthly payments on time. If the original account holder does not pay monthly payments, the late fees not only appear on their report, but they also appear on yours, as well. It might also be advisable to find out if the person you intend on partnering up with has a low percentage of credit utilization.

The simple fact is that you should know that while becoming an authorized user could help you build your credit score; it does come with its risks should the strategy fall flat or go in a way that you did not intend. This is why you should be sure that the original account holder is someone who has a great track record of paying their credit bills on time.

If you're an authorized user on the account, it gets reported on your credit no matter what. Many people have their credit ruined by a spouse or parent going into bankruptcy or not paying their credit card bills. If your name is on any credit cards that belong to people that may not pay their bills, ask them to take your name off immediately!

Chapter 8. What the Lawyers Don't Want You to Know

Listed herein are what credit repair companies don't want you to know and some myths about Credit.

1. It Will Remain on Your Credit Report for Years

A bankruptcy filing will remain a permanent stain on your credit report for seven to ten years, which may have a devastating effect on your potential credit-obtaining ability.

2. Bankruptcy Filing Becomes Public Domain

Bankruptcy is a legal process that ensures it becomes a public record when you file for bankruptcy.

That means that your name and other personal information will appear in court records accessible to the public (including companies, banks, clients, or even potential employers).

3. Filing Doesn't Erase All Debt

Bankruptcy courts have the power to eliminate certain unsecured debts, such as medical bills and credit card balances, but student debt still has to be repaid in full (unless you enroll in any of the loan forgiveness services of the federal government).

4. Filing Is Expensive for Those Without Money

You are filing for bankruptcy because you don't have enough money to pay for payments and debt mounting.

Rates vary by location, but it can take as long as three or five years to conclude a bankruptcy filing, with attorney fees ranging between $2,200 to $3,200 anywhere.

5. Good Luck Finding A Decent Home Loan Any Time Soon

The reality that bankruptcy filers face far harder hurdles in securing a mortgage loan hardly comes as a surprise in a banking world where banks are already skittish about loaning money for a home.

It can take a new bankruptcy filer up to four years before they are accepted for another mortgage loan, according to the Home Buying Institute. Even the Federal Housing Administration needs borrowers to wait at least two years before they can qualify for an FHA home loan after they declare bankruptcy.

There are so many different pieces of information floating around about credit, a lot of which are just myths. We live in an age of information but one of the drawbacks of this is that with so much information, it can be hard to weed out the facts from the myths. Adhering to some of these myths can hurt your credit health.

The first myth that I want to talk about is that having good credit means you have unnecessary debt. I cannot stress enough how untrue this is, it just comes down to understanding how it all works and using it to your advantage, and most importantly, using it responsibly. As referenced early on, having no credit is just as bad as having poor credit, and many people fall into this category because they are always taught from a young age that "credit and credit cards are evil" or "people only use credit when they cannot afford something." This line of thinking is outdated and detrimental when you reach a point where you need to utilize credit. Credit is a great tool, but it requires self-control. Credit cards should be treated as debit cards; only pay for what you can afford, and things you were going to buy anyway such as gas and groceries, and then pay them in full every month to build your credit. If you already spend $60 on gas on your debit card every month, putting that same amount on your credit card and then paying it off does not result in you losing any money or going into debt, it only helps you increase your credit score. However, if you get a credit card and start buying things you cannot afford like expensive clothes and jewelry, the blame falls on you for lacking self-control, not on the company that gave you the credit card.

Another common myth, and reason that many people avoid credit cards in particular, is that you have to pay an excessive amount of money in interest. This is a myth because while credit cards do have an interest, it only applies when you carry a balance on your credit card for longer than one month. As I mentioned before, the goal is only to charge what you can afford, and therefore you can pay your card in full every month. By doing this you will only have the positive effect of building your credit and you will never have to pay any interest.

The third myth is that carrying a small balance on your credit card will help your score. This is completely untrue, as this will result in interest payments due to that revolving balance. There is a myth that lenders may close an account if it has not been used for an extended time. However, using the card often and paying it off will prevent this from happening. It will also prevent you from paying any interest at all which makes it the best method to utilize.

One of the factors of your credit score is each hard inquiry and how they will lower your score. This has sparked the myth that every time you check your credit score, your score will suffer. This is true for hard inquiries, but there is also what is known as a soft inquiry. A soft inquiry is typically when you check your credit information via an online service or through your bank for free. You can check your credit information fifty times per day, and you will see no impact on your score because a soft inquiry does not hurt you. Therefore, it is important to keep an eye on your credit regularly as it will not have any consequences. If there are any mistakes on your report that are negatively affecting you, you can catch them quickly and file a dispute to get them removed.

Another popular myth I want to cover is that having too many credit cards is a bad thing. It goes back to self-control and understanding that you should not be spending money you do not have just because you have the credit available to you.

We talked about how credit utilization is a high impact factor in your credit score, so having several credit cards will increase your total available credit line which will, in turn, boost your credit score. Simply having a larger amount of credit available to you will help you because it shows lenders that you can manage a large amount of money without spending it on things you do not need and cannot afford.

The final myth that you may have heard is that you need a perfect credit score of 850 to get the lowest interest rates when buying a home or car. A score of 850 or anything over 800 is honestly really just good for bragging rights. Generally, a score of 720 and above is what you want to strive for. When you apply for a car loan or a home loan, the interest rate can only be as low as the lender can allow. If the best interest rate they can offer you is around 3%, the person who has a score of 740 will typically get the same benefits as the person who has an 850 score. It is not important to strive for a perfect score, just follow the habits outlined in this book and your score will inevitably rise to high levels.

Chapter 9. How Credit Cards Effect Your Score

Credit cards are a great way to build up your score and get access to all sorts of perks. But credit cards can also be a double-edged sword, especially if you're not paying off the balance every month. If you ever miss out on a payment deadline or accumulate too much debt, your interest rate and credit score will start plummeting like an airplane.

It is about how credit cards affect your credit scores. I break down all the factors that will affect your credit score and explain how to fix them.

Credit Card Payment History

Your payment history is one of the most important factors that determine your score. Your available credit is a part of this, too. A lower amount of available credit on your credit card will hurt you, because it shows that you're using too much of your available credit. If you have a low amount of available credit and a high balance on it, like more than 50% or so, it also looks bad to creditors and your score will drop. On the other hand, if you pay your balances in full every month and keep your overall usage percentage low, then this will be a good thing for your score.

A common mistake people make is paying their credit card balances too low every month. In this case, your available credit will be too low if the amount you use is very low and your balance is high. For example, if you have a $1,000 balance on your card and you pay only $200 a month on it, this will give the appearance to creditors that you are using far less of your available credit compared to someone who has a $10,000 balance on their card and pays twice (or three times) that much in each payment. Be careful to make sure your available credit is not too low.

Credit Card Length of History

The length of your credit history is also very important. The longer the better. All new credit cards you get are going to be added to the total number of all the accounts you've had in the past, and this number will determine your length of history. As long as you only have good credit, this will show that you're a responsible borrower and it will help you get a better score.

Credit Card Credit Limit Amounts

The size or amount of each card's limits also determines the overall total amount of debt on all your accounts, which is part of your score calculation. If you carry a balance on your card that you can't pay off, this is not good for your score. However, if you have enough credit on the card to cover all the balances and do not have any leftover funds, then this will help build up your score as well. Credit limits are determined by each individual lender and can vary greatly from person to person.

Late Payment Fees

Credit reporting agencies like TransUnion and Experian penalize people with high-interest rates for paying late. In fact, they will separate out people who pay late on one charge from those who have a history of paying late everywhere to determine how likely it is that these people will be unable to keep up with their payments in the future. The higher the interest rate, the more likely you will be separated out in the future.

FICO scores are designed to help credit bureaus separate out these late-paying customers by charging them an additional fee. This is not real credit scoring, and it can negatively affect your score if you continue to pay late and do not show that you have started paying on time again.

Maxed-Out Credit Cards

Your available credit limits can also be limited by your maxed-out limits – all the credit limits that you've reached on all your cards combined. When you reach this limit, you may reach a point where paying one card off will cause your available limit to get temporarily reduced or even cut off completely.

The best way to combat this is to apply for a new card and take out a smaller limit. You'll then be able to pay off the old one and have an extra $500 in available credit on it. If you've maxed out the higher limit, you may want to go back down a notch to something lower so that you can remove that card from your credit history and potentially avoid that fee altogether.

Credit Life Experiences (Q Scores)

If you've had several short-term or missed payments, your FICO scores will continue penalizing you for negative information about your track record. This is because they use a proprietary credit scoring system called FICO Q Scores to look at your overall payment history in order to predict how you will behave in the future. The longer it takes you between payments, the more you will be penalized by creditors and credit bureaus.

This is due to another type of scoring system called FICO Q Scores that determines how risky it is for a creditor to loan money to you based on whether or not they think you'll pay them back. PRBC (payment rates, reporting balances, charge-offs) scores are the main components that determine your FICO Q Score, which includes factors such as late-payment fees.

If you have a low FICO Q Score, it means that creditors consider you to be a risk, and they are less likely to try giving you more credit if they deem you to be too risky. This is how your score can actually increase after paying off your balances because it will show creditors that you can be responsible for your payments.

FICO Scores vs. Vantage Scores

Vantage Scores are another type of credit scoring system that was designed by the three major credit bureaus (Equifax, Experian, and TransUnion) as a way to compete with FICO scores from a competitor named Fair Isaac Corp. However, there are some notable differences between the two score types.

The biggest difference is that Vantage Scores are designed to be used by the credit bureaus, not creditors. Therefore, they do not have any real impact on whether or not you get approved for credit cards or other lines of credit. Instead, they are only used to help creditors determine how risky it is for them to lend money to you based on your overall history. A high score in this case does not automatically mean that you'll get a high FICO score.

Differences between FICO Scores and Vantage Scores: Credit Bureaus designed them: Vantage Scores were designed by the three major credit bureaus. They can be used by creditors, but aren't required.

FICO scores are designed by Fair Isaac Corp., which is a third-party credit reporting agency. They are used by creditors.

FICO scores are also used by the credit bureaus as a measure of how risky it will be for them to lend you money, but this has no impact on whether or not you get approved for credit. Credit scoring model: Vantage Scores use a scoring model that is based on 300 to 850 points whereas FICO scores use 300 to 850 points.

Under the new scoring model, Vantage Scores consider your payment history more heavily than credit limits.

Under the old model, FICO scores considered credit limits more heavily than payment history. They are used in conjunction with each other: You need a score that is at least as high as your FICO score to be approved for a credit card.

FICO scores continue to be used by creditors to determine if you are going to get approved for a line of credit, and also if you will get charged interest on it. They use these scores as a way to compare you to other applicants or customers. You are not required to have a FICO score: Your credit history is not scored in the Vantage Score credit scores.

Your payment history is not scored in the Vantage Score credit scores. Vantage Scores are sometimes used by other creditors. FICO scores can be viewed by anyone: The credit bureaus also provide information on your FICO score to anyone who requests it, as well as to your creditors or prospective employers who ask for it. You don't have to pay for having your FICO score checked: You don't get charged anything by the credit bureaus for checking your FICO score, and you also don't have to pay anything if you order a copy of your Vantage Score report.

Free No cost or obligation to order. FICO scores are free, but the credit bureaus charge a fee for providing your Vantage Score. Your report is randomly generated by the credit bureaus and won't contain any identifying information about you, like your name, address, or Social Security number. Unfortunately, some people have reported that the Vantage Score they receive is not a complete and accurate copy of their actual score. Also, note that you don't have to pay anything to check your FICO score.

How Your FICO Score Is Used by Creditors

A creditor may choose to use a different credit scoring system than the one you were given, so they can compare you to others who have applied to be creditors or had existing debts and lines of credit. Creditors are not required to use the same scoring system as the one that is used by third-party credit reporting agencies like TransUnion and Experian. They use their own scoring systems in order to set up their own approval criteria, which won't be designed using the same methodologies or risk assessments as a Vantage Score.

FICO scores are only required to be used in order to meet the requirements of a creditor's own credit policies and practices, such as:

The creditor's minimum credit score requirement for applicants who apply for loans from them; The number of approvals or denials that the creditor gives out; The amount and type of interest that will accrue on a particular line of credit or loan; The amount they will charge you in late fees and penalties if you don't pay off your debts on time; and Any other factors that the lender has decided to add.

For instance, if you want to apply for a credit card with your bank and they decide to use their internal scoring system instead of FICO scores, you might have to pay a $500 deposit to use their card. In addition, there is no guarantee that the card issuer will let you build up your own history with them by making payments on time and paying off your balances without incurring heavy debts.

In this case, they could be using a proprietary credit scoring system that helps them determine if they will grant you access to any lines of credit or not. This scoring system is referred to as an internal scoring model. If they choose to apply your credit history and payment history to their own scoring model, then they will use information from the three major credit reporting agencies, such as TransUnion and Experian.

A large number of creditors are using this method right now. Alternatives like FICO scores are only required by some loan companies and credit card issuers for some types of consumers. This will change over time as more lenders come up with their own scoring systems or switch to another system altogether for consumer approval decisions.

Chapter 10. Debt-Snowball Method

The snowball strategy for credit recovery is a concept that involves first paying off small debts before the large debts to be covered are all that is left. This follows the same idea as creating a snowball, where you have a small ball that eventually develops into a bigger one to start with. In principle, the snowball strategy is perfect because it allows you a chance to see your debts go away one by one. However, this mechanism is not necessarily optimal. Here's a look at how the snowball strategy works so that you can decide if you might want to try something.

The Purpose of the Snowball Method

The snowball strategy is intended to motivate you to continue paying off your debts by encouraging you to see them get paid off. You can at least cross the bill off your list every month if you start with a small credit card. That will make you feel accomplished, and it will give you the confidence you need to continue to pay off your bills. You can pay off another debt over the next few months and then another debt before all you have left one big debt to pay off each month. This will alleviate a lot of your tension, and it should allow you to concentrate more effectively on fixing your loan.

The Downside of the Snowball Method

In principle, the snowball approach is perfect, but it does have a drawback. Large loans demand interest on more money, and that can lead you to pay a lot more over time. You could be shelling out hundreds of additional dollars that you might have avoided by paying big loans first if you leave those loans until the end. You might try to do a reverse snowball strategy, but that might not give you results fast enough to make you feel confident about repairing your reputation. That is why you have to spend more money on this method because it is relatively insignificant in many cases.

How to Use the Snowball Method Effectively

You need to determine the amount of interest you have to pay on various loans if you want to use the snowball approach to your advantage. You must first remember to pay off the 20 percent card if you have five credit cards with a 6 percent interest rate and then one with a 20 percent interest rate. The equilibrium doesn't begin to spiral out of control in that way. Try dividing the payments between the high-interest card and the small balance one if you still want to start with the smallest balance you have. That way, without making the bills piling up at the other end, you can always get everything paid off.

You may also look for some of the high-interest loans to be converted to a low-interest credit card to pay off. You will be able to use the snowball method to its full potential if you do not have to worry about the interest rate. This is rarely the case, but it is something you might benefit from if it works for you. Check out your credit card options to see if there is some way to reduce the interest you pay right now.

Difference between Debt Snowball and Debt Avalanche

By using the debt avalanche strategy, another way to pay off the debt is. This method reverses the order in which you pay off the debt by focusing on the loans or credit cards with the highest interest rates rather than the ones with the lowest balances.

The theory is that you'll save more money on interest by removing loans with the highest interest rates first. However, the actual difference might not be a lot.

If maximizing your savings is your top priority, use the debt avalanche process. But if you like the idea of getting rid of balances more easily by first concentrating on the small ones, use the debt snowball technique.

When Should You Use the Debt Snowball Method?

There is no one-size-fits-all approach to your debt payments. Where one strategy for a friend or family member might work, another may be a better match for you. Here are some situations where the best technique to use could be the debt snowball method:

- Any credit cards you want to close. The debt snowball strategy will help you pay them off quickly if you want to decrease your exposure to credit card debt and those balances are smaller than other loans. You can close the account after that and prevent yourself from once again racking up a balance.

You're trying to reduce the ratio of debt to profits. When applying for new credit, your debt-to-income ratio (DTI) is an important factor, especially with mortgage loans. You'll fully delete them from the DTI equation by removing loans with lower balances, making it easier to get approved for an auto loan or mortgage if you need it.

- You have a hard time remaining inspired. It can be a monumental challenge to pay off debt, and it can be impossible to keep on track if you go without getting rid of any balances for years. You'll begin to see improvement faster in the process by removing your lowest balances first, which will motivate you to stick to your strategy.

During the process, keep an eye on your credit.

Check your credit scores frequently as you focus on paying down your debt to keep track of your success and just to make sure you don't hit any snags. It may stop your progress if you pay off a debt to boost your reputation, and inaccurate or false information is applied to your credit reports. And if you don't catch such stuff early, over time, it might do more harm.

It won't happen overnight to eradicate debt and boost your credit history. But you could save years of time and interest payments if you're patient and stick to your plan, all of which you can invest in working towards practical and exciting financial targets.

Conclusion

For everyone, the snowball strategy is not right, but it might be right for you. If you feel exhilarating after paying off the first debt, give it a try and see. In no time, you will be curious enough to try it again.

Chapter 11. How to Overcome Credit Card Debt?

What is a Credit Card Debt?

When you incur a credit card debt, you actually keep borrowing money every month, and that is why it is also known as revolving debt. But it is only good until you have the capacity to repay them but when you can't, the debt keeps accumulating. When compared to the loan accounts, you can actually keep using your credit card accounts for an indefinite period of time. In simpler terms, there is nothing that the company can seize, like a house or a card, even when you have failed to repay them. But yes, if you are not able to repay the money you borrowed from the credit card, it is going to affect your credit score drastically.

How Is Credit Card Debt Accumulated?

When you get a credit card, you will see that there will be a due date within which you have to clear the entire balance that you have accumulated on your credit card, and if you fail to do so, you will be accumulating debt. There is a term called APR or Annual Percentage Rate and this is a rate of interest that is charged on your debt when it keeps accumulating one month after the other. The APR that you will be charged may not be the same as someone else's and this is because it keeps differing with your credit history, the bank issuer, and also the type of card that you have.

The benchmark fed funds rate of the Federal Reserve and the prime rate of the credit card interests is somewhat tied, and that is the average value. The credit card debt will increase or decrease with respect to any changes in the target rate made by the Fed.

Now, I want to give you an even clearer picture of how this debt accumulates. For starters, there is a minimum payment that you will have to pay every month whenever you use your credit card to make purchases. This payment is calculated based on a certain percentage (with some additional interest charges) of your balance. If you pay this amount in full, then well and good, but if you don't, then you will be liable to interest. So, the interest will increase if you pay even lesser. The reason behind this is that the nature of credit card interests is compounding so the interest keeps accruing. Thus, if you take a longer time to clear off the debts, then you will owe a huge amount of money to the company, which is much more than what you actually owed before.

What Happens After 7 Years?

This is basically a time limit until which a record is shown in a credit report. But there are certain other negative issues that will stay in your credit report even after seven years, for example, certain judgments, tax liens that are unpaid, and bankruptcy.

But you also have to keep in mind that if any debt is unpaid, then it is not exactly going to vanish even after seven years. Even if the credit report does not list it, you will still owe that money to the lender.

There are several other legal ways that can be implemented by lenders, creditors, and debt collectors to collect the debt that you haven't paid. Some of these methods include a court giving permission to garnish your wages, sending letters, calling you, and so on. One thing that you benefit from because of this seven- years rule is that when the debt is no longer visible on your credit report, it cannot affect your credit score. Thus, you can actually have a better chance of gaining back a good score. Another thing to keep in mind is that this seven-year term is only for the negative information on your report and not the position information because they will stay on the report forever. You should keep an eye out after the seven-year mark as to whether the credit bureaus have removed that information or not. They usually do it automatically, but in case they don't then you will have to raise a dispute.

Many people have this question of what happens to their debt if they accidentally die. Well, in that case, it will be your estate that will be used to pay the debt off. Remember that the debt will not be shoved in someone else's hand in your family because whatever money you owe, it is your debt and not anyone else's. And so, whatever you had, like your accounts and assets will then be used for clearing the debt. And after that, if anything remains from your assets, your heir will receive it.

How to Eliminate Credit Card Debt?

Start Eliminating High-Interest Debts First

When you are trying to eliminate your credit card debt, the biggest obstacle that will stand in your way are the ones that carry a very high rate of interest. Sometimes, the rate of interest can even be in double- digits, sometimes as high as 22%. In that case, paying it off can be a really difficult task. But the reason why I am asking you to start eliminating them first because when you will have cleared these debts, you will have a greater amount of money left in your hand at the end of each month.

Another thing that you could do, but only if you have enough credit available, is to apply for a new credit card. But this should be a zero-interest one. Once you get it, transfer the balance to eliminate the high-interest debt. Yes, I know that some of you might be thinking that it is not a sensible thing to do to apply for another credit card and that is why I will be asking you to get it only if you think you have enough self-restraint not to go buy a bunch of stuff that you don't need.

Keep Making Small Payments

Quite contrary to the technique I mentioned above is another technique which is called the snowflake technique. With this process, you will be making small payments towards your debt every time you get some extra cash in hand. Whatever payment you are making, it does not matter as long as you keep paying.

You can pay $10, or you can pay $20 but at the end of the year, you will find that you have reduced about $1000 simply by paying such small amounts almost every day, even if you are paying $2 on any particular day.

People often ignore this method, thinking that it will be only small amounts but you should not make the mistake of overlooking these small amounts as they have quite the power in them. When you are making these small payments, it would feel as if they are not even leaving any dent but with time, they will sum up and cause a considerable effect on your debt.

Preventive Measures to Avoid Credit Card Debt

Have an Emergency Fund

Think about a situation when you have encountered a problem that requires you to spend a lot of money, for example, a car repair or job loss, or medical emergencies. In such a situation, what you need is an emergency fund, but when people don't have that, they resort to credit cards for help.

But why arrive at such a situation when you can build an emergency fund that will cover at least six months' expenses. A fund of this size will help you to figure out any small expenses that crop up overnight. Take your time to build your emergency fund so that you do not have to rely on debt ever.

But Only Those Things That You Can Afford

When you have a credit card in hand, it can get really tempting, and you start buying whatever you think you want. If not, then don't buy it now. Make a goal to save the money required for purchasing that item instead of buying it on credit.

Don't Transfer Balance If Not Necessary

Some people have this habit of clearing their balance with a higher credit card but such repeated balance transferring can actually backfire on you. When you keep transferring balanced without keeping track of your activities, you might end up with an ever-increasing balance and you will also have to clear the fee requires for all those transfers.

Try Not Taking out a Cash Advance

Sometimes, you may be in the moment, and you were not thinking clearly so, you decide to take a cash advance. Moreover, you will have to realize that you are getting into credit card debt if you have started earning cash upfront. The moment you see it happening, you will have to start working on that emergency fund and also tweak your budget.

Lastly, I would like to say that no matter how many measures you take, try avoiding increasing your credit cards unnecessarily because the more the number of credit cards, the more you will have to stop yourself from overspending.

Chapter 12. How to Fix Your Credit Yourself in 9 Easy Steps?

Repairing your credit takes nine steps, each of which will be deliberated in greater detail in the next few pages.

1. Obtain a copy of your credit report from the three major credit bureaus (Experian, Trans Union Corp., and Equifax).
2. Highlight all negative items.
3. Challenge each of the negative items.
4. Request an updated credit report; check to ensure that some of the negative items were removed.
5. Repeat steps 2-4 once every two months until no additional items are removed.
6. Prepare a consumer statement disputing each of the remaining negative items, and request that the Credit Bureau include the statement in your credit file.
7. Request that each Credit Bureau furnish you with the names and addresses of each creditor still reporting a negative entry for your account.
8. Contact each of these creditors and attempt to negotiate a settlement.
9. Request that updated copies of your credit report be sent to anybody who received your credit report in the past six months.

These steps are all based on the rights granted to consumers through the Fair Credit Reporting Act (FRCA). As you implement the steps outlined above do note that the FCRA will not protect any request, challenge, or consumer statement that can be proven to be frivolous in nature.

It is highly unlikely that this charge will be made by a creditor or credit bureau, as they know that your defense can be that you were simply acting according to your understanding of your rights as granted by the FCRA.

Step One: Get a Copy of Your Credit Report

Before you can start to fix your credit report, you must first figure out what it contains. If you still have the credit reports that I suggested you get at the beginning of this book, go to step 2. If you don't have a copy of your report, then do the following:

Contact the three major credit bureaus, Experian Inc., Trans Union Corp., and Equifax Inc., to see which agency has a file on you. You might also want to contact other local credit bureaus, because there may be several different versions of your credit report floating around. It is a good idea to start with the three major credit bureaus and deal with others later.

Although you may save $8.00, in your effort to repair your credit, you don't need any unnecessary credit denials added to your credit report at this time. This is the exact kind of information that you are trying to erase from your file. However, if you don't have the $24.00 necessary to buy all three copies of your credit reports, this is an option.

There are other ways of learning about your credit report. Instead of the letter request, you can call the Credit Bureau and make an appointment to assess your credit file in person. It is advisable that you wait for the Credit Bureau to tell you everything they know about your credit history before you volunteer any potentially damaging information to other parties.

Step Two: Note All Negative Items on the Report

Each Credit Bureau has its own way of organizing its credit reports. Make sure that you read and understand all the information they send on how to read their report. It is up to you to determine which entries are damaging.

Such items may include a different social security number, incorrect name or spelling of your name, wrong addresses, and the excessive number of inquiries, charge-offs, late payments, judgments, or anything else that will keep you from being granted new credit.

Perhaps your record was confused with another customer who has a similar name or social security number. Maybe the negative information is outdated, beyond the seven-year legal reporting limit imposed by the FCRA.

Step Three: Challenge Each of the Negative Items

Send letters to each Credit Bureau, challenging each of the negative items on your report, even though they may be true. The Fair Credit Reporting Act (FRCA) states that any credit item that is challenged by a consumer must be proven by the creditor in order to be considered verified.

If this re-verification is not completed in a timely manner (approximately 30 days) or if the challenge goes unanswered, the affected negative credit items must be completely deleted from your file, never to reappear.

Note: Do not challenge more than four items at a time. Challenging more than four may cause the Credit Bureau to deem your challenge frivolous and deny your challenge.

Your challenges can be based on the argument that:

- You never made late payments to that account
- The account is not yours
- You don't remember the facts as stated on your credit report
- You don't remember applying for the credit card

There may be other arguments applicable to your particular situation. The challenging process works very well because there are many factors working to your benefit:

- Certain negative items cannot be proven because they were legitimately in error and should have never been reported in the first place
- Credit denials are often thrown out by creditors soon after they are received. As such, these items are generally not reconfirmed. Also, if the item is over two years old, there is a good chance that these records are not retained by the creditor.

If you have already paid off the account, the creditor will probably not want to be bothered and will not respond to the challenge.

A creditor might not respond within the time constraints set by the credit bureau in accordance with the FCRA's guidelines, generally about 30 days.

There is also the element of human error that can come into play (i.e., they may lose the challenge report, can't find the proof, things get lost in the mail, etc.) and result in a non-response by the creditor. The end result: the items are removed from your report. So, the odds are in your favor.

Step Four: Receive an Updated Credit Report

Within one month of challenging any negative items, you should receive an updated copy of your credit report (hopefully without some of the old negative items). If you have not received your new report within 6 weeks, call the credit bureau and remind them that you are waiting for the new copy of your credit report.

Step Five: Repeat this Procedure Once Every Two Months

Keep repeating steps 2 through 4 every two months until no additional items are removed as a result of your challenges. If the remaining creditors are determined to reconfirm their claims and continue to do so over and over again, it is time to move on to the next step.

Step Six: Prepare a Consumer Statement

Prepare a 100-word statement of dispute for each of the remaining negative items, and have the Credit Bureau include these statements in your credit file. These statements will show that the situation is still in dispute and that there is another side to the story. You won't be declared unworthy of credit based on these claims, because they are still pending.

Step Seven: Request the Names and Addresses of Each Creditor

Explain to the Credit Bureau that there are still many mistakes on your credit report and that you would like to contact the creditors in question directly. Request that the Bureau send you the names, addresses, and phone numbers of each creditor still reporting a negative entry for your account.

Step Eight: Contact Each Creditor and Negotiate a Settlement

Negotiations between each creditor may differ depending on the circumstances. Creditors of unsecured loans are motivated to settle because after a certain amount of time these accounts are written off as a total loss; any payments would be considered to be "found" money, so you will probably have a very willing negotiating partner.

Step Nine: Ask That They Send Out Your Updated Credit Report

When your credit report is as clean as it's going to get, contact each Credit Bureau one more time. Request that updated copies of your credit report, be sent to all the creditors who received a copy of your credit report within the past six months.

Chapter 13. How to Maintain It and Mindset

Many folks suffer a financial crisis at some point. They may have to deal with overspending, loss of a job, a family member, or personal illness. These financial problems can be and usually are, overwhelming. To make these situations worse, most people don't even know where to begin to solve these financial dilemmas. Our goal here is to shine some light on the strategies to help get youth Accumulating basic consumer debt will chain you into slavery and you could possibly spend your life held down by your own obligations to repay these loans. Who do you work for? I don't care what you say; the real answer is your creditors if you are currently stuck paying the debt. There are many forms of "dumb debt" you can get trapped into. We are all sold images and lifestyles hundreds of times per day to provoke this materialistic behavior.

The person or institution lending you the money is trusting that you have the ability to hold up your end of the bargain, basically. Sometimes, it may seem impossible to live your life without the option to get a credit, but this is what bad credit eventually leads to. Since your ability to repay a loan has been affected, either by the inability to pay or a series of misunderstandings, other lenders will become skeptical when it comes to granting you a new credit.

But how do you get a credit in the first place? What is the process you have to go through to loan money? Well, it all starts with a credit application to a bank or some other party that has the necessary finances. Your application is reviewed and, if they think there won't be a problem with getting their money back, you sign a contract and get your money in no time. This application contains a large amount of relevant information about yourself such as your employment situation, your monthly income, and other credits or obligations like rent, for instance. The application you submit to a lender is used to obtain a credit report from one or several reporting agencies, depending on how much money you need. These two documents are given scores and, if your score is enough, you'll get the money you need. If not, your application will be rejected. If you don't fall into any of these categories, then a judgment call has to be made by the person or institution providing the credit. The more "good credit" criteria you meet, the more likely it is that you will get your credit.

However, there are several things that you must consider before you put yourself into the category of citizens unaffected by bad credit. First of all, the lenders look for certain things in your application, such as an up-to-date credit report and no late payments on your other financial obligations. They are interested to see if you've had a job for more than a year and have a stable income, as well as a stable residence. They also evaluate the situation of your utility and phone bills and appreciate it if you include information about additional credit cards or other types of cards. It is not only banks and money lenders that look at this type of information. Sometimes, if you want to get a new job, your employer will conduct this type of research too, so maintaining a good credit is crucial in these troubled times we live in.

What type of credit should you get? That depends on what you plan to do with the money. The most used types of credit are secured and signature credits. For smaller loans, there's no need for that, as no institution would like to end up with a store of household items, so they lend you money or issue a credit card in your name simply based on the strength of your credit so far.

There is hope; you as the borrower have many options to get rid of debt. You can take advantage of budgeting and other techniques, such as debt consolidation, debt settlement, credit counseling, and bankruptcy procedures. You just have to choose the best strategy that will work for you. When choosing from the various options, you have to consider your debt level, your discipline, and plans for the future.

The Good Debt

Some people find it hard to live debt-free at least they will have some debt to pay off. While some debts are discouraged, good debt is considered as the money you borrow so that you can pay for things that you really need or things that increase in value. On the flip side, bad debt is one that arises from things that you only want and often decreases in value.

Of course, debt isn't a bad thing; it's just how you use the money that matters.

For a good debt, you will always have a good reason to justify it, and a developed plan for paying it so that you can clear the debt as quickly as possible.

An individual with good debt will also have the cheapest methods of borrowing money. They will do this by looking at the borrowing method, rate of interest, credit amount, and charges that are appropriate to them.

Sometimes, it may imply a deal with the least possible interest rate, but sometimes, it may not.

Examples of good debt

Paying for medical care. There is no fixed amount of money to borrow to ensure your loved one stays healthy. You can manage to pay off the money you borrow, but it is impossible to replace a human life. If a person requires expensive treatments to ensure they remain healthy, this would be an acceptable debt, no matter what.

Borrow money for education. When you apply for a student loan debt, you aren't making the wrong decision. In general, people with college degrees earn more income in their life than those without a degree.

And applying for a student loan so that you can support the education of your child defeats the idea of using your savings. After all, you cannot borrow money to pay for your savings. Multiple government programs provide low-interest student loans, and you can always cut student loan interest on your taxes.

Taking out a mortgage on a home. Taking a loan of this amount can be overwhelming, but purchasing a house creates ownership in something that will house you, and generate some retirement money. Even while you struggle to clear your debt, you may consider it an advantage to put any available liquid cash as a deposit, though it may not be the right choice.

A home mortgage interest is cut on your taxes, and the rate of interest is lower on your home loan than on the credit card. In other words, it is important to have money to pay for other expenses instead of credit.

Though purchasing a house was initially considered a strong, future-proof investment, certain homeowners do find themselves on the wrong side on their home mortgage loan. They owe banks more than the value of their homes. However, strategic planning, purchasing only what you can afford, and maintaining low interest by having good credit may allow you to purchase a home that one day you will own completely.

Buying a car. If you don't have public transport in your area, or you cannot manage to get someone with whom you can carpool, then you may have to consider buying a car. An auto loan can either be "good" or "bad," but the main thing is to ensure that the auto loan is a good debt, so look for the lowest possible rates on your loan. In addition, you need to make a large down payment while ensuring that you remain with some cash on hand just in case you need it.

Your best goal should be to go for a used car model instead of a brand-new one, possibly saving yourself thousands on the sticker price and the interest that is paid throughout the loan.

Business loans. While this may not be seen as good debt, borrowing money to begin a business or expand a business is perhaps a great idea if the business is thriving. After all, you need money to make more money, right?

Sometimes, you may have to borrow capital to employ new people, purchase a new device, pay for advertisement, or even develop the first new widget you designed. The point is that you borrow this money to expand the business or increase income, then this will count as good debt.

What is Bad Debt?

Bad debt is that which depletes your wealth and isn't affordable. Plus, it provides no means to pay for itself.

Bad debts may have no realistic repayment plans and usually deplete when people buy things on impulse. If you aren't sure whether you can repay the money, then don't borrow the money because that will be a bad debt.

Examples of bad debt

The credit card debt. A typical household in the United States has a balance of more than $10,000 on their credit card every month. However, the debt usually increases faster than we may realize and is always used to purchase things that we want instead of need. It is easier to think that you can afford something using a card than paying it with cash.

Borrowing from a 401K. When you ask for money from a 401K program, you will need to chat with the IRS, and if you aren't using the money to purchase a home, you will need to pay the loan in five years. If you fail to pay it back, you risk being charged with a severe penalty. Also, the interest that you pay on the loan will get taxed twice.

You can't get a loan to fund your retirement. For that reason, borrowing money from your retirement plan to use it to pay for anything that isn't part of retirement is a bad idea. You will be putting your retirement at risk when you get a loan from a 401k, so don't make this mistake.

Payday loans. It may appear easy to borrow money from payday loan firms, but it is hard to pay it back. These companies offer loans with very high interest rates. The companies take advantage of the fact that many people need that money. As a result, borrowing a small amount may end up costing you a lot.

Payday loans aren't considered the worst kind of debt that you can take on. If you really need a short-term loan, it is better to go for a cash advance on a credit card rather than borrow money from these firms.

Using consolidation or settlement strategies to pay down debts

Debt consolidation is another strategy that can be used to manage your debts. It involves combining two or more debts at a lower interest rate than you are currently at.

But it is worth doing your research and making some phone calls to see if there is a company that's willing to work with you. If you can lower your monthly bill to a manageable level, at an interest rate that's reasonable, that can make all the difference in handling your debt.

Like many strategies, you have had the option of settling your debts with companies for decades. Lenders always want as much money as you can give them versus being shafted for the entire amount in a bankruptcy. It is just that consolidation and settlement options rose in popularity during the recent financial crisis making it appear in more articles and news pieces than ever before.

If you have savings to pay off your debts, then start with the most expensive. Otherwise, utilize settlement options where you are able to reduce the amount owed if you pay a certain amount right now. As long as the account shows paid in full, with a strong payment history, your scores are going to increase. It doesn't matter if you needed to use debt settlement strategies to make the debt end. It just matters that you have paid the debt off instead of letting it go into arrears.

Chapter 14.   How to Remove Extra Names and Addresses from Your Report?

It's not a secret that you have to work hard to get the best credit score possible. It's also not a secret that different businesses use your social security number and address for identity verification. When you are doing your due diligence, you may want to remove these addresses and names from your report if they're showing up on your credit report unnecessarily.

This post will cover what information can be removed from your report, how long it can take, what companies this removes information from, and other considerations like whether or not it affects the accuracy of loans.

Contact Your Credit Reporting Agencies

The first thing you want to do is contact the credit reporting agencies. (Equifax, Experian, and TransUnion) Ask them how to remove information that's on your credit report but that isn't yours. For example: your neighbor's name on file with collections, someone else's collection, or extra addresses. They will likely guide you to their removal process and may show you a form or a link to fill out. You may be able to call them as well if they offer phone support for the removal of such information.

Most of the time the process is simple and just takes a few weeks. You may have to provide documentation of why you want to remove information from your credit report.

If you want the removal to be processed for free, you will need to contact each of the companies and follow their instructions as to how much documentation they require. The minimum amount of documentation required is generally $10 per account/file or $35 for all three. In general, showing a lack of usage of your address and social security number will suffice as evidence that the information shouldn't be on your file in the future.

Note: If you wish to dispute anything that is on your file, such as an item going from good standing (not being charged off) to bad standing (charged off), these are handled separately. So, make sure you contact all three credit reporting agencies and follow their instructions on how to dispute.

How Long Does This Take?

The process can take anywhere from a few weeks to over a year depending on the nature of the information being removed, the number of accounts, and the amount of documentation required. In general, it's not uncommon for removal to be processed within a few months.

A good rule of thumb is that it will take longer if you need to provide extensive documentation like paying off collections balances or demonstrating no usage. It may also take longer if an item is disputed or you're having other issues with your report. There are also certain criteria that need to be met or removed from your report in order to prevent having the issue reappear at a later time.

What Companies Does This Remove Information From?

This will vary depending on what information you're trying to remove from your report. If you want to remove addresses and names, this information is shared among Equifax, Experian, and Transunion. Therefore, it will be removed from all three companies' files. The same applies if you want to remove an old address or name from collections accounts or other bad standing items like charge-offs or late payments. These are available to all three credit reporting agencies and therefore the removal process is likely very similar across all three companies.

If you are trying to remove accounts, collections, or items that don't impact your credit score (for example, old open accounts) you will not be able to remove this information from all three companies. This is because Equifax and TransUnion will not share certain information with Experian. This means that you can only get eliminated from some of the reports at one or two of the companies. If you are trying to get removed from Equifax's report, for example, the removal process will likely be different than if that information was on Experian's report.

If you are looking to have an account, collection, or other information removed from all three companies' credit report, you will need to make sure that is listed only on one of the companies' report.

How Does This Affect the Accuracy of My Loans?

This can be a complicated question since each lender is different and uses varying criteria to determine your score. Some lenders will only pull one of the reports if they are available for a specific address or social security number. Others may not care at all and pull all three if they have access to them. Generally speaking, most lenders use all three credit files and pull from each one equally in order to determine your credit score accurately.

If you are trying to get removed from all three companies, it's possible that your score could be negatively impacted when the removal is processed. This is due to the fact that if profiles are removed, any lender that pulled all three files would not have access to them in the future. Therefore, the information for those specific accounts/profiles won't be available when determining your score. As a result, your score could decrease for a short period of time as other lenders are trying to evaluate your request.

The most common instance that may cause your score to decrease is if you are trying to remove an address that is used by a lender. This is because they may not be able to access the account or profile for the new address if it was previously listed on all three reports. However, since most lenders use all three equally, this shouldn't have a negative impact on your score long term.

What Are the Best Ways to Get Removed from Credit Report Information?

If you want the removal procedure to go as easily as possible, there are a few things you can do to make it go as swiftly as feasible.

1. Identify Which Companies are Requesting the Removal

Make sure that you identify which company you are dealing with so that you know what information they have access to. This is important because it will affect the process of making sure that information is removed from the correct accounts or profiles. As mentioned above, there is a good chance will be able to remove all three reports with one removal request. However, you may need to make specific requests if certain accounts or items only appear on one of the reports.

2. Focus on Removing "Current" Information First

If you have ongoing collections or other items that can be removed, focus on getting those items removed first rather than focusing on past accounts (like old charge-offs). The reason for this is because the new collections or accounts will be listed on the credit report longer than a paid-off account. This means that it will be harder to get removed from the account later on if you previously had it removed but then added it again later.

3. Removing Old Information is Only Necessary If It is Impacting Your Loan Process

The final thing to keep in mind when removing information from your credit file is how this information relates to your loan process. As mentioned above, the removal of old collections and paid accounts won't have any impact on your current loan process if you are making a large purchase today. However, if you are making a home purchase in the near future, it is important that the reports do not show collections or accounts that are more than a few years old.

Having good information on your credit file will help your loan process go smoothly and quickly. However, having old accounts or collections can create negative information for some lenders and may slow down the loan process from you getting to closing on your new home. Therefore, it is important to focus on removing collections and older accounts first. Depending on how particular your lender is about their accuracy, getting a little creative with removing troublesome information can be beneficial to your overall loan process.

Chapter 15.   Delete Inquiries Like the Pros

An inquiry is when a creditor, employer, or insurance company requests to view and examine your credit reports via TransUnion, Equifax, or Experian. You have soft inquiries and hard inquiries, a hard inquiry is when you give consent to any potential creditor to pull your credit reports, and too many hard inquiries will hurt your score. Soft Inquiries are also referred to as a soft pull, this is when you check your own credit, or credit card companies want to look at your score to solicit you for pre-approval offers.

Current creditors often perform soft pulls to issue periodic credit line increases. These acts are both documented by the credit bureaus, no need for you to worry about soft pulls; they will not hurt your credit score no matter how many times you check your own credit. You can opt-out to prevent others from looking at your reports through soft pulls. Hard inquiries will be kept on your credit report for a period of up to 25 months. Allowing too many creditors to pull your credit within a short period of time will damage your chances for new credit as each inquiry can cost you 3-5 points of your fico score, it is best to have no more than 5 inquiries reporting at a time on each credit bureau. Applying for too many accounts will result in you looking too thirsty to obtain credit. The longer an inquiry sits on your credit report, the less it impacts your fico score, but too many recent inquiries will get you automatic denials in the computer underwriting systems of most banks and credit card issuers.

It is never a good idea to request any forms of credit before you plan on financing any big purchase, especially a mortgage. Every point counts when you are looking for low-interest rates on long-term loans. Another way to control inquiries is to understand which credit report will be pulled by certain creditors; you can even direct certain creditors to pull from a bureau of your favor by freezing the others and applying by phone. Perhaps you have the highest score with Equifax, and you know a specific lender that pulls both Equifax and Experian, it would be wise for you to freeze Experian that has the lower fico score, and this allows easy access to your Equifax. Applying for enough credit over the years, I created my own database of which credit bureaus lenders pull from, which can also depend on your city and state. You can also legally freeze and unfreeze any of your credit reports at any time online or over the phone.

How to Delete Inquiries like a Pro

It is very common to see files of clients that have 10, 15, or even 20 inquiries on each credit bureau. Either they have let a car dealership or multiple car dealerships run their credit through multiple banks, or they crossed their fingers and applied for any and every credit line they could think of. Either way, with computers processing most applications, this can be an automatic denial for many credit products, especially for credit cards and loans from prime issuers. Too many recent inquiries only show lenders you are desperate for credit, and banks only lend money to those who appear to not really need it. For those who do have many inquiries, you don't necessarily have to wait 2 years for them to fall off; you can actually question their legitimacy and request that the credit bureaus delete them.

A Permissible Purpose includes the use of the report for the following reasons:

1. With the consumers written authorization.
2. In connection with the extension of credit as a result of an application from a consumer.
3. In connection with the collection of a consumer's account.
4. In making a decision to hire or promote a consumer who has given written permission for the use.
5. In connection with the underwriting of insurance as a result of an application from a consumer.
6. In response to some other legitimate business need arising in connection with a business transaction initiated by the consumer.
7. To determine whether the consumer continues to meet the terms of an account.

With this being said, it is tough for any credit bureau to prove that you actually gave permission for a creditor to view your credit report, especially without a physical application.

Once they forward the dispute to the furnisher, that creditor really doesn't have any interest in going back and forth with you over this disputed inquiry. Once again, they have bigger fish to fry; they have to worry more about those who actually do owe them some money. Most consumers apply online or on the phone these days for accounts, so it is impossible for these furnishers to provide any physical proof that you actually did initiate the inquiry. If you write and send your dispute by mail for multiple inquiries, make sure it is with a demand letter to the credit bureaus first; it can become costly sending certified mail to multiple creditors individually. You can formulate your letter and ask for these 3 simple things:

1. Permissible purpose.
1. Proof that the consumer initiated the inquiry.
2. Written authorization.

Those who pulled your credit cannot provide these three things unless you have an account attached to the inquiry, and if so, I advise that you count your blessings for the approval and don't try to remove it.

Remember, anytime you are disputing inquires you are standing on the grounds that an application in your name was unauthorized, if for any reason you are being ignored or they refuse to delete, you can send a 605B Identity Theft related letter with the support of an automated police report listing all inquiries you are disputing. If you call to dispute, depending on who helps you over the phone, they will want you to report the inquiries as fraudulent, then forward you to the fraud department anyway. After disputing the inquiries, you will have what is called a fraud alert on your credit file as a result. A fraud alert just means that before any credit can be extended to you in the future, they will first have to go through all the necessary steps to assure that you are who you say you are, and not someone attempting to use your identity. If a fraud alert is placed, just remember you will be better off applying for additional credit in person or over the phone until it comes off or you request to delete it by phone that will take up to 48 hours to process. Fraud alerts last 90 days and extended fraud alerts stay on your credit reports for 7 years. Adding your permanent phone number to your fraud alert is the most convenient way to go, I personally suggest that you remove the fraud alert right after you get the inquiries deleted if you plan to submit any applications after. Fraud alerts can help protect your credit otherwise.

With any resistance from the credit bureaus, you can also dispute your inquiries one by one directly with the creditors. They usually won't put up a fight, I prefer to dispute with the credit bureaus first as it is less time demanding than reaching out to every single furnisher responsible for reporting an inquiry if there are many. If for some reason you missed a step or just can't get the results you need, you can threaten or actually sue the furnisher of the inquiry for the violation of section 604 of the FCRA, this violation can reward you with a fine from the defendant. You will never get all the way to court for a matter like this, but as always, have your paper trail.

*Do not repeatedly apply for credit and dispute your inquiries just because you know how, you want to do everything in moderation to not abuse this tactic for yourself.

"Making more money is not always the answer; some people make 7 figures but still live paycheck to paycheck."

Chapter 16. The FUQ'S (Frequently Unasked Questions): Things Everyone Should Know About Their Credit Score.

Frequently Unasked Questions

In life, questions are more important than answers. The reason is that you get a clearer understanding of things when you learn to ask the right questions. So, I called this the Frequently Unasked Questions because this section deals with questions that people want to ask about but is not really what everybody asks, so they assume it is not necessary to know. Just like I have mentioned over and over again in this book, the best way to understand the credit score world is to never assume you know it all. Keep asking and researching, find out information about your credit report, credit score, and how banks make use of your credit history in deciding on your loan requests. Here, I will show you questions you may already know the answers to, but I will take my time to properly explain them and also questions you might have never even thought of yet, but I bet you they will be useful in the long run.

What is the catch in having a good score?

Everyone should be interested in having a good score as this has several advantages. Some of which are, for a case where you would like to take a loan out, it will help you get very favorable conditions. This also supports you in winning the contract for a new apartment. Many property managers do not take the risk and look for solvent tenants in particular who pay the rent on time. These are just a few benefits, amongst many.

What factors influence my credit rating?

When you're shopping, either online or in a fixed shop or supermarket, there's a lot to consider. "Zero percent financing" sounds like a good idea, but bear in mind that this is also a loan. This is not often concluded with the company, where a product is to be bought, but with a cooperating bank. Because "zero-percent financing" is a loan, it is only available to consumers with good credit ratings and has an impact on your score. Paying attention to some hidden costs such as processing fee which is also very important. Either it is online or on the ground, when ordering from mail-order companies, endeavor to pay invoices on time. Otherwise, your score can be affected negatively. A corresponding score means that you can't order on account.

What is the importance of performing scoring procedures?

The scoring procedures are performed most times when you want to borrow. Even if you're using the "zero-percent financing," a scoring is carried out nevertheless. Moreover, scoring plays a major role if a company is to provide a service before you pay for it. This often happens with mobile phone contracts or shipping dealers a lot. However, the score value does not only determines whether a loan is granted to you but on what terms and conditions as well. A customer with a good score will obviously receive better terms and conditions than a customer with a bad one. They can, therefore, be able to ascertain that the customer will repay the credit without hitch or difficulty. This then means that scoring procedures help companies, banks, and as well as service providers, in particular, to assess the risk of a business and be able to hedge it.

How do they compose my personal score?

The scoring process involves, on one part, one's personal data and historical experience on the other. From this, a phantom score is prepared by means of mathematical-statistical methods, allowing indications of the future behavior of the "scanned" person. Including the data and experience values, already included in the evaluation, the socio-demographic data (such as gender, age, the payment experience, known address, etc.), or contract data (such as the number of accounts and credit cards). However, the specific composition of scoring is a whole lot different for each scoring provider and is not made public.

Are credit rating and credit scoring the same?

No, they aren't. Score values deal with the creditworthiness of a group of people. However, the term "creditworthiness" or credit rating is known as the solvency of an individual or a company.

What does score entail?

Scoring helps to predict the behavior of groups of people with similar characteristics. Mathematical-statistical methods are used to calculate scores of a group of people and hence a statement is obtained on the risk of payment default of those people. The assumption most times is that people with the same characteristics will also tend to behave the same manner. Hence, this suggests that scores do not evaluate the creditworthiness of a single person, but rather predict the payment behaviors of a group of people to which a specific person belongs to. In the scoring process, empirical values from the past are applied to make deductions on similar events that play out in the future.

What time was credit scoring born?

Around the late 1950s and early 1960s, banks in the United States of America started working together by sharing their customer data, which included account balances and payment histories especially.

This method was, at first, limited to just small communities.

However, as of the 1970s, several large companies emerged as leaders in credit reporting.

In 1970, the American Congress initially approved the Fair Credit Reporting Act (FCRA) in order to control the manner in which credit verification companies handled personal consumer information. This was the first step towards the regulation of the sector.

In the early 1980s, loans, requests, detailed personal information (including social security numbers, addresses, date of birth), and also payments that are still the basis of the credit valuation were electronically stored.

Why credit scoring? Why does it exist?

The credit history reporting system aids banks in not lending money to customers who have already been over-exposed and tagged as bad payers.

Until less than 80 years ago, the banking sector was a different experience entirely. Then, if you want to borrow money, you had to go into a bank branch and convince a manager one-on-one to grant you a loan. A proof of your income would have been requested from you as well as personal references who could guarantee your reliability. Back then, most loans were taken care of by guarantees, meaning that good collateral had to be offered to pay off the loan.

The commonest example of a loan guaranteed today is the loan for buying a property. In this agreement, the property is still the one that acts as the collateral.

With time, the high availability of credit cards as a comfortable electronic purchasing tool has also cleared the unsecured loan. And even if the unsecured loan were more profitable to banks, it was still very risky because there would be no guarantee for the bank to repay the sum paid if the debtor does not repay the loan.

Because of this, the credit scoring system came into play and was created to enable banks to have a central source of information on prospective customers.

What are the other factors that influence your credit scoring?

Yes, some of which is the average age of your current accounts, recent funding requests, and any collateral that has been pledged against your assets.

Each of these makes up about 10-15% of your credit score.

The longer you have the current account, the better. Also, try to limit the credit requests to no more than two at least every six months. When you have too many credit requests in a short time, it can decrease your credit score as it suggests that you are in desperate need of money.

However, there is an exception for those whose credit requests are of the same nature. This will indicate that you are making an evaluation of a particular expense.

If it happens that these requests occur within a month or so, it will be generally accepted as one request.

What does the personal information in my credit scoring consist of exactly?

Your credit scoring contains all information about you, which includes your name, social security number, address, and information about your financial assets, such as payments histories, balances, and loan applications.

Your credit report majorly contains detailed information on recent activity on your financial accounts. This includes:

- **Credit requests:** whenever you request a credit, either you have been approved or not.
- **Open loans:** the data will have the bank, the loan amount, the loan opening date, the monthly payment amount, and the payment history.
- **Use of credit cards:** data includes the ban, credit limit, account opening date, payment history, and the monthly payment amount.
- **Closed accounts:** a closed account remains on the report for a maximum of up to seven years.
- **Public accounts:** include judicial decisions and bankruptcy declarations.

How do you know you are doing a good job? How do you measure your progress?

As much as your credit report contains all information about your credit history, your credit score remains the best way to measure your progress in building your credit. Your credit score is referred to as the numerical summary of all information contained in your credit report within a particular time. It is the number that lenders and creditors use to decide whether to approve your requests and what interest rate to charge.

There are sites on which you can get your scores free of charge, some of which are creditkarma.com and creditsesame.com. You can also get your for-FICO number for an affordable fee at myFICO.com. This FICO score, especially, is the one most creditor use.

This way, you can regularly monitor your credit score and update yourself on the changes that occur over time in your credit history.

How can I repair my bad credit scoring?

It's the same method for building a good one! Paying bills on time and staying away from debts. The best way to repair your credit is to pay your bills, reduce the level of debt per time and limit demand for fresh loans.

It would take about one or two years of responsible credit management to see your credit score improve exponentially. There are no shortcuts. Stick with this and you will see the change you desire

Chapter 17. How to Protect Your Credit and Credit Monitoring?

Knowing everything you can about the credit card game is important. Almost everyone has a credit card, but few people know how to use it correctly. Chances are you are reading this book because you have already made financial mistakes and you want to fix them. Don't apply for a credit card before you've read the terms. There's more to choosing a credit card than picking a design or a credit card issuer. You need to evaluate the card on other factors as well. Consider what kind of card you want. Do you want a rewards credit card, a regular credit card, a student credit card, or a card that you can transfer a balance to? How you are planning on using a credit card is also something that you need to consider. If you are going to be carrying a balance on the card, look for a low interest rate. Find out what the annual percentage rate (APR) is on the credit card, and also what the grace period is that you can pay your balance in full before you are charged an additional finance charge. Finally, find out what the yearly fees on the card are and what the reward structure is on the card.

Don't Use Credit Cards for Necessities

Do not use your credit cards to pay for things like clothes, gas, and food if you have the cash on hand. Most people find themselves on the road to debt by using their credit in place of cash. If you are using your credit card as a way to build your credit, it can be wise to use it in place of money, as long as you are making sure that you are putting the same amount of money aside from your bank account to put back on your credit card.

If you are using the money on your credit card for groceries and still spending the money that you have in the bank, you are going to find yourself in debt very quickly.

Don't Get into The Habit of Only Making Minimum Payments

By paying only the minimum amount required on an account, you are only putting off the debt that you owe, which also increases the amount of interest you are going to accrue on the account. Usually, minimum payments are only the amount of interest gained on the outstanding balance so you won't even be making payments toward the actual principal debt.

By paying as much as possible toward the balance, you are helping to decrease the amount of the principal debt, which in turn decreases the amount of interest you will pay in the long run.

Don't Use Credit for Things You Can't Pay For

Don't live above your means. If there is an expensive item you want but don't need, it's important to recognize that if you don't have the money for it now, you probably won't have it anytime soon. Wait until you have the money to pay for your purchases before you acquire them.

However, sometimes you need to make a high-ticket purchase because there is an emergency, for example, your fridge dies, or you need a new furnace.

In an emergency, it would be appropriate to use your credit card as long as you are making it a priority to pay the balance on your credit card back down.

Don't Close a Credit Card Account Without Knowing How It Is Going to Impact Your Credit Score

Your credit score may suffer if you close a credit card account. Avoid closing accounts with balances or accounts you've had for many years that have made up a great portion of your credit history.

When you look at your credit report, you are going to be able to see how long you have had a credit account open. It is not a smart idea to close your credit card if you have had it for ten years and it is in excellent standing, especially if all of your other credit cards are newer.

Let Your Creditor Know If You Won't Be Able to Make Your Monthly Payment on Time

Ignoring the situation is not going to make it go away. If you are unable to make a payment on time, contact the company, and discuss available options.

Many times, they will work with you to adjust your due date and waive late fees if you know this will be a one-time problem.

Keep an Eye on Your Utilization

Remember, you want to keep the utilization below 20%. That means that you are going to want to try to keep the amount on your card within 20% of your credit limit. Not only is this going to keep your balance low and more manageable, but it will also help to keep your credit score high. Ask for a Lower Interest Rate If you have maintained or improved your credit and begin to receive offers from other institutions offering you a lower rate than you are currently paying, contact your creditors and ask if they will lower your interest rate.

Review Your Credit Card Statement Thoroughly Every Month Don't assume that everything that is on your credit card statement is accurate. Read through every transaction and ensure that your last payment was applied properly, that you were charged correctly for all your purchases, and that there are no unauthorized charges on your account. Report unauthorized charges to your credit card company immediately and dispute errors within sixty days of them occurring.

Chapter 18. Reach Your Financial Freedom

Financial freedom is a concept that people love to think about but rarely feel like they can reach.

What Is Meant by Financial Freedom?

Financial freedom has no set definition. However, it typically means that you are living comfortably and saving for retirement and in general. It can also mean that you have an emergency reserve set up. In general, financial freedom can mean whatever you want it to mean for you. For example, a prior college student may not think that financial freedom includes paying off all their student loans. This is because, at least in this day and age, a college student who needs to pay their way realizes they will always be paying off their student loans. However, they might feel that student loans are the only debt they should have. Therefore, being able to pay off credit cards or medical bills leads them to financial freedom.

Some people might feel that financial freedom indicates they have absolutely no debt or loans. This includes them having paid off their mortgage and any car loans. They might also feel that in order to reach financial freedom, they need to be investing in a CD, bond, or even in the stock market.

Other people may feel that financial freedom means they are no longer tied down to a job. They are able to live off of their savings or a passive income, and they are able to retire and enjoy life through traveling.

Credit Cards and Financial Freedom - Is It Safe?

One of the biggest questions people have when it comes to financial freedom is whether they can have any credit card accounts in their name. While you may not owe anything on your credit cards (in fact, you might only owe one which you pay off in full every month), is this still financial freedom? In general, this is completely determined by your definition of financial freedom. However, if you ever find yourself not being able to pay off your credit card every month, this is not financial freedom. In most cases, financial freedom does mean you no longer have any debt, or at least that you are free from unnecessary debt, such as credit cards.

Most people are quick to state that financial freedom and credit cards do not go together simply because they are not safe with each other. This is due to the fact that it is often easy to fall back into thinking you can pay the amount off everything each month and then you become unable to do so. In general, people who reach financial freedom feel that credit cards allow for more of a trap and keep them from ever reaching financial freedom.

However, other people who feel they have reached financial freedom state that as long as you can manage your credit cards wisely, they can be included with your freedom. Some of them also advise that you set up a financial freedom plan. Within this plan, you will state your conditions for using a credit card. Of course, you need to be self-disciplined enough to follow your condition.

The Best Habits to Help You Reach and Protect Your Financial Freedom

When it comes to financial freedom, there are dozens of habits and tips that people provide in order to help you reach your financial freedom. It is important to note that because financial freedom can vary depending on the person's definition, some of the tips and habits might work for you while others may not. You need to find the ones that work best for you, not the ones that other people say are the best. Therefore, I am going to give you a fairly large list as I want you to make sure that you can find some of the best habits and tips so you can not only reach financial freedom but also protect it.

1. Make a Budget

Making and keeping a budget is one of the first steps everyone should take while heading towards financial freedom. Even though you might find yourself changing your budget now and then, as you will add or delete bills or receive a different income, you always want to follow it. Not only will this help you in reaching your financial freedom but continuing to follow your budget will also protect your financial freedom.

Furthermore, creating a monthly budget can make sure that all your bills are being paid and you know exactly where your money is going. For example, you will be able to see how much money you spend on groceries, gas, and eating out at restaurants. This will help you know where you can decrease your spending, which will allow you to save more. There are a lot of great benefits when it comes to creating and sticking with a household budget.

2. Set Up Automatic Savings Account

If you work for an organization that will automatically place a certain percentage of your check into a savings account, take advantage of this. It gives you the idea that you never had the money to begin with, which means you don't plan for it and you won't find yourself taking the money out of savings unless you need it for an emergency. Furthermore, you can set up a separate savings account where this money will go. You can make it, so you rarely see this account, however, you want to make sure that your money is deposited, and everything looks right on your account. But, the point of this account if you do not touch it, even if you have an emergency. Instead, you will set up a different account for an emergency basis.

The other idea to this is you pay yourself first. This is often something that people don't think about because they are more worried about paying off their debt. However, many financial advisors say that you are always number one when it comes to your finances. While you want to pay your bills, you also need to make sure that you and your family are taken care of.

3. Keep Your Credit in Mind Without Obsessing Over It

Your credit score is important, but it is not the most important thing in the world. People often fall into the trap of becoming obsessed over their credit score, especially when they are trying to improve it. One factor to remember is that your credit score is typically only updated every so often. Therefore, you can decide to set time aside every quarter to check on your credit report. When you do this, you not only want to check your score, but you also want to check what the credit bureaus are reporting. Just like you want to make sure everything is correct on your bank account; you want to do the same thing for your credit report.

4. It Is Fine to Live Below Your Means

One of the biggest factors of financial freedom and being able to maintain it is you can make your bills and comfortably live throughout the month. In order to do this, you need to make sure that the money coming into your home is more than the money going out. In other words, you want to live below your means.

This is often difficult for a lot of people because they want to have what other people have. They want to have the newer vehicles, the bigger boat, the newest grill, or anything else. People like to have what their friends and neighbors have. However, one factor people don't think about is that their friends and neighbors probably don't have financial freedom. Therefore, you want to take a moment to think about what is more important for you. Would you rather be in debt like your friends or you would rather have financial freedom?

5. Speak with a Financial Advisor

Sometimes the best steps we can take when we are working towards financial freedom is to talk with a financial advisor. They can often give up information and help us with a budget, ways to make sure that we get the most out of our income, and also tell us where we might be spending more money than we should. Furthermore, they can help you figure out what the best investments are, which are always helpful when you are looking at financial freedom. At the same time, they can help you plan for your retirement, which is one of the biggest ways you will be able to remain financially free.

6. Completely Pay Off Your Credit Cards

If you are high-interest credit cards, which is often the case, you want to make sure that you pay these off every month. Therefore, your credit card spending should become part of your budget. What this means is you don't want to use your credit card for whatever you feel like. Instead, you want to create a list of when you can and when you can't use your credit card. For example, you might agree that it is fine in emergency situations or during Christmas shopping. You might also feel that you can use it during tips because it has trip insurance attached to it. Whatever you decide, you want to make sure you follow.

You also want to make sure that you pay off any high-interest loans. When it comes to loans that are lower in interest, they won't affect you too much.

7. Track Your Spending

Along with making sure you follow your budget; you also want to track your spending. There are several reasons for this. First, it will help you make sure that your budget is on track. We often forget about automatic bills that are paid monthly or don't realize how much we really spend every month. These factors can make our budget off, which can cause an obstacle when you are working to reaching and keeping your financial freedom.

Fortunately, there are numerous apps available for download, many of which are free, that will help you to quickly track your spending. Some of these apps include Mint or Personal Capital. These apps typically give you all the information you need and will automatically tell you how much you are spending and how much income you still hold at the end of the month. Most of these apps will also give you charts to help you see your spending habits in a different way.

8. Make Sure to Keep Your Mindset

This is a mindset that you will want to continue to have while you are living financially free. With this mindset, you will not only feel grateful for where you are in life, but you will also remember where you once were. This will help you work towards protecting your financial freedom instead of falling back into credit card debt.

Of course, you can adjust your mindset the way you want to once you reach financial freedom. However, you will want to make sure that you keep your mindset positive. After all, a positive mindset makes you believe that you can accomplish anything.

Chapter 19. Template Examples and Simulations

Template 1

This is the primary format that we will invest some energy in. It will incorporate the entirety of the various parts that you need to get the message to the correct gatherings, and it is quite basic. Recollect that this is only a layout, and we can go through and utilize this as a guide or a blueprint. On the off chance that it doesn't by and large coordinate with what you need, you can roll out certain improvements, or you can decide to utilize one of the different layouts that we will have access to.

Name

Address

Telephone Number

Record # (make a point to incorporate this on the off chance that you have that data).

Name of the Company Contacting/Point of Contact Person

Important Department

Address

Date

Dear [Include the name of the credit revealing office or utilize the name of the contact party in the event that you approach this information]

I'm composing today to practice my entitlement to scrutinize the legitimacy of the obligation your office claims I owe, compliant with the FCRA, Fair Credit Reporting Act.

As expressed in Section 609 of the FCRA, (2) €:

"A customer revealing office isn't needed to eliminate precise harsh data from a purchaser's record except if the data is obsolete under Section 609 or can't be checked."

Just like my right, I am mentioning confirmation of the accompanying things:

[This is the place where we will list any of the things that we are hoping to debate, including the entirety of the record names and numbers that have been recorded with your credit report]

Furthermore, I have featured these things on the joined duplicate of the credit report I got.

I demand that all future correspondence be done through the mail or email. As expressed in the FCRA, you are needed to react to my debate within 30 days of receipt of this letter. In the event that you neglect to offer a reaction, all contested data should be erased.

Much obliged to you for your brief regard for this matter.

Earnestly,

[Add your mark to this part]

[Print your name here]

See appended; [This is the place where you will rattle off the entirety of the archives that you will connect with this letter]

*Make sure that you join duplicates of your verification of personality, including your introduction to the world date, name, SSN, and your present street number. You additionally need to join a duplicate of your credit report, ensuring that you featured the entirety of the significant things to make it simpler for the invested individuals to perceive what you are discussing.

Template 2

There are a ton of times when the primary format that we talked about will be sufficient for your necessities and can assist you with completing the entirety of the work. Then again, it could be conceivable that you need to discuss the debate in an alternate way, or you just didn't care for the arrangement or something different about the other layout that we went through. That is okay. The accompanying layout will be the one that we can work with too. It discusses a ton of the very issues that we did above however will have a couple of different parts added to it to make this work too. The third format that we can work with incorporates:

Name

Address

Telephone Number

Record # (make a point to incorporate this in the event that you have that data).

Name of the Company Contacting/Point of Contact Person

Important Department

Address

Date

Dear Sir or Madam

I'm writing to practice my entitlement to debate the accompanying things on my document. I have caused a note of these things on the joined duplicate of the report I to have gotten from your organization. You will likewise discover connected duplicates of reports that help to show my personality, SSN, birthdate, and current location.

As expressed in the FCRA, or Fair Credit Reporting Act, Section 609:

[This will be the segment where we incorporate a couple of pertinent statements that depend on what space of Section 609 you might want to debate at that point. You can return to the past section to perceive what a portion of these statements is about, or you can go to the FTC's site to get the authority report that has the specific verbiage that you need. Recollect that you need to note which of the sub-segments you are citing from as well].

The things that I wish to question are as per the following:

- 1. [This is the part where you will incorporate however many significant things as you can. You can have up to 20, yet attempt to just work with the ones that bode well for you].
- 2. [Keep as a main priority that the subtleties will be the most significant with this one. You need to incorporate the name and the quantity of the record, as recorded on your credit report]

These are [inaccurate, wrong, unverified] because of the absence of approval by various gatherings that is needed by Section 609. I have appended duplicates of important documentation.

I would see the value in your help with researching this way inside the following 30 days. As needed by the FCRA, on the off chance that you neglect to do as such, all previously mentioned data/questioned things should be erased from the report.

Genuinely:

[Add your mark to this part]

[Print your name here]

See connected; [This is the place where you will drill down the entirety of the records that you will append with this letter]

*Make sure that you append duplicates of your verification of personality, including your introduction to the world date, name, SSN, and your present postage information. You likewise need to connect a duplicate of your credit report, ensuring that you featured the entirety of the significant things to make it simpler for the invested individuals to perceive what you are discussing.

Template 3

We have investigated some truly genuine instances of the format that you can use with regards to working with Section 609 and ensuring that you can get the credit offices to delete a portion of the awful stuff that is on your reports and causing you a ton of issues en route. In any case, we will investigate a fourth layout that we can use also.

You will see that this one will be really like what we have done in the last two, yet there are some various approaches to introduce the data and various words that are being utilized also. We should investigate this model and perceive how it very well may be comparable or not the same as the other two layouts that we are working with:

Name

Address

Telephone Number

Record # (make a point to incorporate this in the event that you have that data).

Name of the Company Contacting/Point of Contact Person

Applicable Department

Address

Date

To the responsible party in question,

This letter is a proper debate as per the Fair Credit Reporting Act (FCRA).

Endless supply of my credit report, I have discovered that there are a few off base and unconfirmed things. These have adversely affected my present capacity to get credit, and have given pointless shame and bother.

As I am certain you know, it is my right, as indicated by Section 609 of the FCRA, to demand a legitimate examination concerning these errors. Specifically, I am referring to Section 609 (c) (B) (iii), which records "the privilege of a purchaser to question data in the document of the buyer" under the "model synopsis of the privileges of shoppers."

All things considered, coming up next are things I wish to question on my credit report:

1. [This is the part where you will incorporate however many applicable things as you have. You can do up to 20. Ensure that you incorporate the name and the number that is recorded on each record on this report.]

I have additionally featured the entirety of the things that are pertinent to the appended duplicate of the said credit report.

As expressed in the FCRA, you are needed to react to my debate within 30 days of receipt of this letter. In the event that you neglect to offer a reaction, all contested data should be erased. I have connected all the significant documentation for your audit. I thank you ahead of time for your brief reaction and goal of this issue.

Truly

[Add your mark to this part]

[Print your name here]

See joined; [This is the place where you will drill down the entirety

*Make sure that you connect duplicates of your evidence of character, including your introduction to the world date, name, SSN, and your present street number. You additionally need to connect a duplicate of your credit report, ensuring that you featured the entirety of the applicable things to make it simpler for the invested individuals to perceive what you are discussing.

Template 4

This will be a somewhat unique sort of letter than what we saw previously. This will be significant in light of the fact that it assists us with following up on the off chance that we have not heard a single thing from the other party. Recall that we are allowing them 30 days to go through and give us a reaction or the like, or they naturally need to take that off their reports. The 30 days starts when they get the letter you send, not when you compose it or when you send it. This is another motivation behind why it is critical to go through and get it sent through confirmed mail, so you have a precise date close by.

At the point when the 30 days are finished, the time has come to do a subsequent letter. This will be the point at which you let the organization realize that the 30 days are finished and that you anticipate that things on your report should be deleted and finished as quickly as time permits. That is the reason we will work with the accompanying to assist us with composing the subsequent letter that we need.

Name

Address

Telephone Number

Record # (make a point to incorporate this in the event that you have that data).

Name of the Company Contacting/Point of Contact Person

Important Department

Address

Date

Dear Sir or Madam

My name is [Your name], and I contacted you a little while back in regards surprisingly report. This letter is to inform you that you have not reacted to my underlying letter, dated [insert date]. I have repeated the provisions of my question beneath for your benefit.

[This is the place where we will embed data from the letter we expounded initially on the contested things. Incorporate questioned account names and numbers as recorded on your credit report.]

Area 609 of the FCRA states that you should explore my debate inside 30 schedule days from my underlying letter. As you have neglected to do as such, I generously demand that you eliminate the previously mentioned things from my credit report.

Any further remarks or questions can be coordinated to my lawful delegate, [insert name], and I can be reached at [insert telephone number].

Genuinely

[Add your mark to this part]

[Print your name here]

See joined; [This is the place where you will rattle off the entirety of the reports that you will connect with this letter]

*Make sure that you connect duplicates of your evidence of character, including your introduction to the world date, name, SSN, and your present street number. You additionally need to append a duplicate of your credit report, ensuring that you featured the entirety of the pertinent things to make it simpler for the invested individuals to perceive what you are discussing

Conclusion

Your credit report is the most important report you have. It can prevent you from obtaining a mortgage, car loan, or another type of financing for a new home or car purchase. You should take steps to protect your credit and check your credit report on an annual basis to look for any inaccuracies that may be affecting your score.

As you become older, having a strong credit history can make things easier for you since lenders will be more inclined to give money to someone who has a track record of managing their finances responsibly and not missing payments or incurring late fees. If not handled properly, mistakes in your past could haunt you for years to come.

Taking a proactive approach to your credit will help you rectify any inaccuracies that are discovered and take the necessary steps to maintain a positive credit history. If you want to make a change in the way your credit score is calculated and influence what information is reported, you must fill out and submit the proper forms to the major credit-rating agencies (Equifax, Experian, and Trans Union) that track your financial activity. These forms are called "opt-ins" or "opt-outs" and can be obtained from each of the three major credit bureaus. Apply for an extended fraud alert or a security freeze on your account if you detect anything improper with your credit report.

When you move, it can be difficult to have information in your credit report updated by your creditors. This is because you have little control over the information they provide about your payments. In effect, the new notice of address change that you send them will be ignored. The best way to ensure that your information is correct is to initiate a "credit freeze." This prevents all lenders from seeing or changing your credit report without first getting permission from you. A credit freeze does not prevent the lenders from opening an account for you or extending credit from them, but ensures that no changes are made without your approval.

www.ingramcontent.com/pod-product-compliance
Lightning Source LLC
Chambersburg PA
CBHW081442220526
45466CB00008B/2484